# enough is enough

## A biblical call for moderation in a consumer-oriented society

## JOHN V. TAYLOR

AUGSBURG PUBLISHING HOUSE
MINNEAPOLIS, MINNESOTA

ENOUGH IS ENOUGH

First United States Edition 1977

Copyright © 1975 SCM Press Ltd.

First published by SCM Press Ltd., London

Library of Congress Catalog Card No. 77-72456

International Standard Book No. 0-8066-1584-2

MANUFACTURED IN THE UNITED STATES OF AMERICA

# Contents

# To Grow or Not to Grow

'I wish you wouldn't squeeze so,' said the Dormouse, who was sitting next to her. 'I can hardly breathe.'

'I can't help it,' said Alice very meekly: 'I'm growing.'

'You've no right to grow *here*,' said the Dormouse.

'Don't talk nonsense,' said Alice more boldly: 'You know you're growing too.'

'Yes, but *I* grow at a reasonable pace,' said the Dormouse: 'not in that ridiculous fashion.'

*Alice's Adventures in Wonderland*

### Prophets of doom

Three years ago economists, ecologists and social scientists started a violent debate which has continued ever since. In January 1972 *The Ecologist* devoted a whole issue to *A Blue-Print for Survival*. It appeared over the name of thirty-three scholars, mostly scientists and obviously sincere. It was based largely on a book which the authors had seen, though it was not published until two months later: *The Limits to Growth*. This had been written by Dennis L. Meadows and his colleagues at the Massachusetts Institute of Technology under the auspices of an informal international association of industrialists, scientists, economists and educators, calling itself the Club of Rome.

*The Limits to Growth* derives its arguments from an intricate world-model which shows the inter-play of such factors as the global growth of population, of industrial capital, of environmental pollution, and the exhaustion of the world's non-renewable resources of minerals, chemicals and fossil fuels, and the insuperable limit to food yields.

The conclusions of the study were deeply pessimistic.

1. If the global figures for population and for industrial output continue to increase, as at present, in a geometrical progression – or, to use the jargon, exponentially – then natural resources which are non-renewable will become exhausted during the next century. Agriculture and industry will slow down more and more until food production becomes inadequate for the human race.

2. If that model is corrected by new discoveries of non-renewable resources and by recycling wherever possible, then a rising pollution of the environment will bring about a drastic decline in food production early in the next century.

3. If, besides solving the problem of natural resources, pollution is statutorily reduced, then industrial production can have a longer lease of life, but the population explosion will exhaust the food supplies.

4. Even if the population is levelled off and the research enables us to double our food yields, then the exhaustion of the land, the eventual depletion of resources and the slower but still inexorable accumulation of pollution must ensure the collapse of the human life-system by the end of the next century.

One is reminded of the words of a much earlier and greater prophet of doom: 'It will be as when a man runs from a lion, and a bear meets him, or turns into a house and leans his hand on the wall, and a snake bites him.' But the Massachusetts Institute of Technology, like the prophet Amos, does not leave us entirely without hope. The conclusion of the argument, we are told, is that we must immediately plan – hopefully the date 1975 is proposed – to level off the upward curves of population growth, industrial output, pollution and, a little later, *per capita* food production in order to achieve a stabilized global equilibrium.

There is obviously no surer way of arousing the emotions of economists than to suggest that the highly developed countries of the West should deliberately stop the growth of capital investment, slow down industry's consumption of raw materials, and set about educating the citizens to expect a levelling-off of the standard of living. To say these things is to challenge the basic assumptions of the economic theory by which we have lived since the 1930s and, with rather less awareness, for far longer than that.

The authors of *The Limits to Growth* anticipated a widespread disagreement with their figures and an angry dismissal of the solution they proposed. So in the end they seemed to be ready for their opponents to drive a coach and horses through their date-lines and statistics, if they could only be persuaded to accept the fact that this spaceship, Earth, is a home that is already becoming almost too small for us:

> There may be much disagreement with the statement that population and capital growth must stop *soon*. But virtually no one will argue that material growth on this planet can go on forever. Man can still choose his limits and stop when he pleases . . . The alternative is to wait until the price of technology becomes more than society can pay, or until the side-effects of technology suppress growth themselves, or until problems arise that have no technical solutions. At any of those points the choice of limits will be gone. Growth will be stopped by pressures that . . . may be very much worse than those which society might choose for itself.[1]

It is even possible that their startling facts and figures were intended as shock tactics to dislodge Western man at least from the assumptions that have governed his outlook and his aims for many centuries:

> A whole culture has evolved around the principle of fighting against limits rather than learning to live with them. This culture has been reinforced by the apparent immensity of the earth and its resources and by the relative smallness of man and his activities. But the relationship between the earth's limits and man's activities is changing.[2]

Whatever we may conclude about the nature of the limits that are inevitable, we have to recognize that all the curves on the graph are shooting up – expectation of consumer goods, consumption of energy and of raw materials, pollution and, of course, population. Our present situation of rapid material growth, which encourages every family to expect as of right an ever-expanding surplus, is, in the light of man's long history, so abnormal that one knows it has to cease. Sooner or later the curves have to flatten out. And if the *quality* of our children's life in this world is any concern of ours, then, in the industrialized countries at least, the sooner the better.

So the heated debate began. First came the voices of those who were a good deal more pessimistic than *The Limits to Growth*. Dr Aurelio Peccei, the founder of the Club of Rome, agreed in principle with the report, but suggested that some major crisis – a collapse, a breakdown, an explosion in world society – may well occur much sooner than the report suggests, because, according to him, it ignores the socio-political limits of growth, and concentrates only on the physical and economic limits.

## What about the Third World?

Even such an optimist of technology as Andrew Shonfield, formerly Chairman of the Social Sciences Research Council, drew attention to the inappropriateness of a global moratorium on capital growth while the under-developed nations were struggling desperately to industrialize their economies. In a special supplement of *The Observer*, he expressed his fear that, though technology may enable the wealthy nations to solve the problem of their own population growth and the ravaging of raw materials by the end of this century, these safeguards will be limited to the Western world by sheer expense, and will only sharpen the inequalities between rich and poor nations. 'I think,' he says, 'the rich may find themselves more beleaguered, more cut off from the rest of the world by the beginning of the twenty-first century.' And he also comments: 'Looking after the environment for the sake of one's grandchildren is a rich man's preoccupation.'

That argument was advanced many times by some of the 1,200 delegates from 112 nations who met at Stockholm in 1972 for the first world conference on the human environment. There were even those who suggested that, true or false, ecology is the red-herring that Mr Nixon dragged across the trail of the anti-war protestors in 1970, and that the rich nations are grasping at it now to justify their evasion of their most obvious responsibilities towards the poorer nations during the Second Development Decade.

A Korean, Pyong-Choon Hahm, put it this way not long after that Stockholm consultation:

> It is a supreme irony of world history that the concern for environmental pollution on the part of the industrially advanced portion of the globe is now being thrust into the path of industrial development of the underdeveloped world which has finally succeeded in forging a commitment to ethnological salvation of its own. It is as if the industrialized world had purposely taunted and humiliated the underdeveloped world into abandoning its non-industrial cosmology in favour of a more European and technologically oriented world-view in order now to frustrate and disappoint the Third World's new commitment to development . . . Unless and until the actions of the rich countries demonstrate clearly their determination to de-industrialize, the poor countries' reaction would only be that they will industrialize first and control pollution later when they can afford to do so.[3]

It strikes me as even more ironical that the industrialized countries should at this moment evince such new concern for the freedom of poor countries to pursue capital growth through industrialization. One smells no mean rat when this concern is produced as an argument for maintaining growth at all costs in the industrialized countries. I shall be returning to the needs of the poorer, struggling nations in a later chapter; so at this point I want to examine this argument only so far as is necessary to de-fuse it.

It is said that an expanding world population demands the production of more and more goods, and of more and more wealth, to keep pace. An unrestrained growth economy, it is said, will eventually eliminate the poverty of the world's poor since, as more and more goods are produced, more wage employment will become available to more people, and also the prices of all the things that make life easier and fuller will come down within the grasp of the proletarian or peasant consumer all over the world. Even though at present most of the new wealth is concentrated in the rich countries, it will eventually be more evenly distributed.

But, in fact, none of the evidence seems to bear this out. That is not the direction in which the curves are moving. Growth economy is interested in profits, not products; it seeks to reduce labour costs, not to create jobs. As a few of the poorer countries begin to industrialize and knock on the doors of the rich countries, bidding them open their markets, they are met with a cold rebuff in the form of tariffs and quotas. There is something extraordinarily cynical in the argument that the best way to feed the poor is to pile even more upon the rich man's table in the hope that bigger and better crumbs will fall from it.

It seems to me that those who use this argument are deliberately closing their ears to the appeal for a *greater* altruism as the only route to a global security and well-being.

Those who quote the needs of the poorer nations to discredit all the findings of *The Limits to Growth*, seem deliberately to ignore those passages which place a special responsibility upon the rich nations. The report says:

> The greatest leadership will be demanded from the economically developed countries, for the first step towards such a goal would be for them to encourage a deceleration in the growth of their own material output while, at the same time, assisting the developing nations in their efforts to advance their economies more rapidly.[4]

But even more altruism than that is called for. As Andrew Shonfield admits in the comment I have quoted, only the 'haves' will be able to afford the massive correctives that are needed to combat pollution and restore a sound ecology. Unless they, and they alone, accept responsibility for applying environmental controls *throughout the globe*, they must not espouse a plan that depends on spreading throughout the world their kind of industrial and consumer growth.

That kind of enlightened, altruistic common-sense must seem impossibly idealistic to all the politicians, industrialists and trade unionists who still put their trust in an economy oriented towards continuous growth. Let them at least be honest, and not pretend that their present policies will eventually raise the standard of living in the poorer nations. They will do nothing of the sort.

### Who makes up the rules?

The poorer countries, many of them only recently emerging from the colonial rule of the industrial powers, have lived, for the most part, by being the agricultural plantations and raw-material deposits of the rich countries. Their value to those rich countries depended on their supply of cheap labour, raw materials and foodstuffs. The classical argument of the liberal schools of economics, with which I am often confronted, says that world prices must be fixed by the simple law of supply and demand, and that countries trade with each other because each of them possesses certain comparative advantages over the others in the cost of producing and distributing goods.

Now the laws of supply and demand and of the open market have a somewhat ruthless efficiency which a Christian conscience may shrink from applying in every case. In spite of that, however, the poorer nations would be only too thankful to be allowed to operate under those laws of economics. But when, in recent decades, have they ever been allowed to do so? Again and again the powerful nations interfere with these laws and bend the rules to make sure of winning every game. Prices are fixed in defiance of the law of supply and demand by the monopoly buying of a poor nation's total tea or sugar crop, by an unscrupulous use of bargaining power, and by other manipulations which have nothing to do with a straightforward competitive market. So the less-developed countries are condemned to be for ever the suppliers of raw materials for the industrialized nations and so remain in continuous dependence upon them and their dictates. If they do manage to set up the beginnings of an industrial

7

infra-structure of their own, there is no corresponding reduction of the same industries in the rich countries which enjoy so many more opportunities of diversification; on the contrary, their efforts to enter the market are frequently blocked by quotas, tariffs and the deliberate manufacture of synthetic substitutes by the industrialized powers.

The results of this ruthlessness have been summed up by an African, J. F. Rweyemamu:

> The share of the developing countries in total world exports declined from 30·4% in 1938 to only 19·1% in 1966. In the first half of the 1960s, total world exports grew at an average annual rate of 7·8% and exports of developing countries, excluding oil exports, grew at an average rate of only 4%. Whereas the average prices for primary products exported from developing countries have decreased by 7% since 1958, those for primary products exported from developed countries have increased by 10% in the same period.[5]

As an example of this, Dr Roy Billington has pointed out that ten years ago Ghana could buy a tractor from overseas by exporting one ton of cocoa. To buy a tractor today she has to export about five tons. The problem is illustrated by what happened at a price-fixing conference for cocoa a few years ago. The larger producers, such as Brazil, were trying to get a minimum price of 27 cents per pound, but the largest and most militant consumer, the United States, insisted on a minimum price of 20 cents. Most of the other importing countries were ready to agree on a compromise of 23 cents; but America refused to change her offer and, because she takes over 25% of the world production, was able to get her own way.

What happens in cocoa also happens in textiles. At the Annual General Meeting of shareholders in the great Carrington Viyella textile firm in 1972 a small protest demonstration was staged because the firm had called for larger trade barriers against textile imports from developing countries such as India and Pakistan, though its profits for the preceding year were up by over 500%.

How seriously can we take the oft-repeated concern of the governments of industrialized countries over the debilitating malnutrition in most of the poorer nations, when every year all ten million tons of the Peruvian anchovy fisheries' catches, which amount to one-sixth of the world's total fish production, are taken by the rich countries and fed to their livestock and poultry?

How are we to evaluate the £40 million which Britain allocated to India in aid in 1968 when in the following year it was announced that a tariff of 15% was to be imposed on imported cotton textiles from India? Unless a British government can be persuaded to change this policy, the effect will seriously reduce India's capacity to earn by trading with us. The justification, of course, is that tariffs are necessary to protect the cotton industry of Lancashire. That is a fallacy. The real problem is how to protect the livelihood of Lancashire people. The new tariff has not been much help to them, since the Report of the Textile Council (1969) says that rationalization and automation are likely to put 50,000 of them out of work by 1975.

Readers in England will remember the documentary TV film which showed the appalling conditions and the outrageously low wages of the tea-pickers who work for British firms in Sri Lanka. Yet, if the *New Internationalist* is to be believed, Brooke Bond made £228,000 from its Sri Lanka estates. This is what 'investment' in the poorer countries often means. But now it is being replaced by a more reliable use of cheap labour, as one after another of the industrial enterprises of Western Europe come to rely on up to 80% immigrant labour. They no longer want to face the expense and upheaval involved in running Western-style businesses in the developing countries, with all the schools, swimming-pools and churches that expatriate staff expect. It is much simpler if men grown desperate for want of work in their homelands should come and work for them in the European Community, often without a vote and with no prospect of bringing their families to live with them. The personnel director of the German lorry firm, MAN, is quoted as saying: 'It is inconceivable that we could continue running the factory without large amounts of new foreign labour.'

So the idea that the continuous capital growth of the wealthy nations will eventually enrich the poor, struggling nations also, has been called 'a shabby lie', and in all soberness I am bound to agree. The truth, as I see it, was very well put in a paper published two months after the Stockholm conference by the British Society for Social Responsibility in Science.

Within the world community, even the poorest UK citizen belongs to the rich minority – less than one-third of the world's peoples who consume three-quarters of its non-renewable resources. Even with a great increase in the amount of recycling, there will never be enough of these resources – oil, non-ferrous metals, phosphates – for the whole world to consume at the rate the rich now enjoy, and if the rich continue their growth in consumption there will not even be sufficient for the poor two-thirds to build up the basic infrastructure of industrialization. The Third World countries are too poor to be able to buy and use more of these resources now. How will they be able to afford the price in money and in technical expertise when they are scarce? We believe that the developed countries must reduce their consumption of non-renewable resources, their pollution of the air and the sea, and their exploitative trade and investment policies. The Third World countries should be allowed to work out their own ways to prosperity, ways that are certain to differ from those that the rich have chosen up to now. They might well have a lot to teach the rich about alternative technologies and social organization, more appropriate to life on a small and crowded planet . . . The present system functions to benefit certain groups at the expense of others, and those now living at the expense of generations yet to come. A social system is needed in which the purpose of production and economic activity is not profit but the satisfaction of genuine needs.[6]

### New nations offer new values

That last quotation strikes a different note. We have become accustomed to seeing the African, Asian, Latin American and Island countries in the role of suppliants calling for our charity, or at least a greater generosity. But now we have to get used to a very different tone of voice. At a conference of Asian Christian youth in the summer of 1973 the cover design of their programme showed the outline of a Coca Cola bottle superimposed upon a simple map of Asia, and underneath were the words: 'Lead us not into imitation.'

Fortunately – and this is where the champions of limitless growth are most wide of the mark – fortunately a growing number of the leaders of Asian, African, Latin American and Island nations are beginning to doubt whether their own future welfare has to depend on a spillover from the affluence of the highly developed countries. In China a quarter of mankind is moving forward in a quite different direction. Raw-material production is labour-intensive, geographically dispersed and ecologically less damaging. Their whole technology is advancing rapidly, but the determining factor is not profit but total social welfare.

Many of the poorest struggling nations are making a conscious and deeply-felt rejection of the values and attitudes which the growth economy of the industrialized nations seems to embody – violence towards nature and depreciation of personal relationships. Our 'get out of my way' philosophy is being judged more and more harshly by the rest of the world, and they would sometimes prefer to live with their problems than to solve them by our technological methods.

Of course the rich Chinese business man in Hong Kong wants an E-type Jaguar. Of course his wife wants a washing machine in their high-rise apartment. Of course the poor working families on the opposite hillside want a cheap TV set to compensate the drab fatigue of their evenings. It would be surprising if they did not all feel those wants when so much has been spent in advertising to ensure that they do feel them. Yet none of this alters the fact that more and more of the poorer peoples of the world reject the spin-off of our Western economic growth as a panacea for global well-being.

Idealism is very fragile, but its rejection of cynicism is sometimes surprisingly violent. Writing in the *New Internationalist* about the ordinary Africans in the liberation movement in what was once Portuguese Guinea, Basil Davidson, whose books have done so much to keep us aware of the struggles of the people of the Portuguese territories, put this very forcibly:

> If the mental and physical liberation of these African peoples under Portuguese rule had depended on the accumulation of things, it could have made no progress . . . As it is, these peasants and their national movements have shown that the development of themselves, of their individual understanding, of their collective ability to work together, of their capacity to free themselves from foreign rule, of their vision of a just society in the future, could and can unfold while they themselves remain in rags and tatters, hungry or in peril, lacking nearly all the things that are otherwise supposed to be required by a 'developed' life . . . No ministries here, no motor cars, precious little paper-work, an absence of everything save bare necessities: often not enough of those, sometimes desperately not enough. But people, people . . . people arguing, people learning, people deciding, people acting together. The development of people is different from the growth of things.[7]

In their powerlessness the poorer nations are ready to make use of the economic weapons which they have so often seen wielded in the hands of the industrialized countries. The Arab oil embargo at the end of 1973, which took us by surprise, was only the first indication that the poorer countries may soon begin to realize the power of acting together (and incidentally, why did most of us miss the point that while the Arab countries asked 3p more on every gallon of petrol they sold, the British Government still took $22\frac{1}{2}$p in excise duty?). Julius Nyerere has talked about 'a Trade Union of the Third World'. We should be getting our minds used to the idea of a coffee crisis, a cotton embargo or a rice ring. We ought to learn to regard these, when they come, as a natural development towards that more just distribution of the world's wealth to which we have so often paid lip-service. Fairer shares in the family of mankind will begin to happen when the prices of goods go up in our shops and wages are *not* lifted to match them. Quite simply there is no other way. This society of excessive consumption exists within, and indeed thrives upon, a larger society of excessive need. That is the context of our plenty, and our plenty is not making things better, but worse. Let us have no more talk of our abundance overflowing to the rest of the world. Even if that were the ultimate outcome, long before it is reached the excessive consumer habits of the fat nations will have bled white the environment off which all the nations have to live. So, in the long view, it may be better for us all when the poorer nations begin to organize and dictate their terms.

### The debate goes on

After that diversion into the objections raised against the arguments of *The Limits to Growth* by some spokesmen of the poorer nations, let us return to the other aspects of the debate. Naturally it raged furiously for a year and more. The most important corporate riposte came from a team at Sussex University who in 1973 produced *Thinking About the Future*. They showed in considerable detail that the statistical basis of *The Limits to Growth* was seriously unreliable because it did not make serious allowance for the application of scientific correctives and new discoveries. This, of course, was the argument of Dr Aurelio Peccei; but while he used it to open up the possibilities of even earlier doom, the Sussex University team used the argument like Mr Micawber: 'Something will turn up!'

It is a perfectly sound argument against any conjectural projection of present trends into the future without allowing for unforeseen change of a radical kind. By plotting a graph of the expansion of the monasteries throughout the Middle Ages we might easily have concluded that nine-tenths of the British people were celibates today. But such a calculation would not have allowed for such a change as the dissolution of the monasteries.

*Thinking About the Future* reminds us that, if we are to talk about the exhaustion of non-renewable resources, we must allow for new areas of the earth's surface to be prospected, new deposits discovered, the conversion of coal to various uses, the working of lower grade ores and oil shales, the recycling of waste and the invention of substitute materials.

If one is to discuss the rising level of pollution we must allow for the certainty that it can be reduced or counteracted by scientific means as soon as governments insist upon industry being responsible. At the same time we must recognize that we are only beginning to tackle the problem and know very little about the effects of anti-pollutant processes upon the soil or the seas.

If we see danger in the increasing inadequacy of food supplies, then we should take account of the real possibility of developing almost as much new arable land as is in use at the present time.

And finally, if we think it is the population explosion that spells our doom, we must remember with cool heads that population can be controlled.

But, in all seriousness, can it? – or can it be controlled in time?

It took a million years to produce the first billion human beings. It took only a hundred years to produce the second billion, by the 1850s. It took only fifteen years to produce the fourth billion, by 1973. And the next forty years will add to the world's population more people than the whole history of mankind has done to date. It is already far too late to do much about that. But unless we are to shelve our responsibility, and rely upon the most hideous 'act of God' of all time to solve the problem for us – and even then we shall in fact be responsible for what happens – the governments of the world simply have to unite in insisting on achieving Zero Population Growth, that is to say, one birth for each parent is the limit, however many times each may get married. 'Two is enough, three is too many' should now be a matter of conscience for every married couple, or it will soon have to be made a matter of law. And because the observance of such a rule is so much easier and more readily understood by the citizens of the wealthy countries, they should consider applying an even stricter limit, or making up their total of two by adoption instead of by birth.

Let no one think that the poorer countries are the only ones in which population is a problem. Because of the extraordinary success of medicine in postponing mortality, practically no country in the world is in sight of a stabilized population. But naturally it is in the vastly greater insecurity of the under-developed countries that it is so much harder to persuade families to limit the numbers of their children. Dr Roy Billington, whom I have already quoted, has written on this score:

> Paradoxically, the most effective way to secure the adoption of family spacing may be by providing better child health care. If mothers see that their children are passing safely through the dangerous first 5 years of life, they will be ready to consider having smaller families.[8]

1974 has been designated 'World Population Year', but I have not heard of radical decisions taken by any government as a result of this. Yet now is the time to act, for the largest child-generation of all time is already growing up to marriageable age. Even if Zero Population Growth were imposed by law this year in every country of the world, it could take another sixty years to stabilize the population of the globe.

### Are we serious?

This massive challenge to the good sense of the human race, this question about its very survival, leads me to ask why so little is still being spent on the scientific research and the humdrum fact-finding without which we are still only floundering in the dark.

When naming the new Executive Director of the United Nations Fund for Population Activities which stands behind the organization of World Population Year, the Secretary-General, Kurt Waldheim, paid particular attention to the need for more detailed knowledge. Without this the governments of the poorer countries, or of the richer ones for that matter, are not going to be willing to commit large funds and risk considerable popular disapproval for the sake of a hit-or-miss experiment. We know the facts, roughly, of the number of children born each year in each country, and they are so alarming that most people simply put them out of their minds in order to avoid despair. People generally will not face these facts until some thoroughly tested proposals for dealing with the problem are presented to them.

These proposals are almost bound to be unpalatable, including, as they must, not only a simple and universally usable method of contraception, but deterrent taxation on families with more than two children, and possibly, even, a resort, when necessary, to compulsory sterilization. Of course there will be enormous resistance to such interference with the private lives of individuals, but unless governments set out the alternatives in such harshly practical terms as these, no one is going to take this unprecedented problem seriously. And, however one looks at it, there are far fewer moral objections to be raised against sterilization than there are against widespread abortion.

These are problems to be tackled, together or separately, by biochemists and gynaecologists, lawyers, social scientists and moral theologians of different faiths. And churches should be demanding the setting up of such a research programme immediately.

But that is only one sphere in which research is desperately needed. We need far more knowledge about the side-effects of fertilizers and pesticides and of all the anti-pollutant measures which are being proposed. We need a completely fresh approach to the scientific farming of the seas, with a new law-book to bring the oceans and the seabeds under internationally recognized control. We need cool-headed measurements of heat, the heat generated by our development of energy resources, and the long-term effects of raising the temperature, ever so slightly, of the atmosphere or the seas. And, together with this, we need far more research into the possible uses of solar energy. We need a more positive study of the particular factors which the Massachusetts Institute team chose to highlight in mainly negative terms, in order to arrive at some irrefutable conclusions about the carrying capacity of 'this space ship, Earth'. If the astronomical sums of money that have been squandered on the Vietnam war and on the exciting but, in every sense, lunatic expeditions to the moon, had been devoted instead to these life-giving programmes of research, we would be in a far better position for taking responsibility for the events of the coming century.

This was the gist of an imposing address given in Canterbury Cathedral in August 1973 by Sir Kingsley Dunham, President of the British Association for the Advancement of Science. He recalled that the authors of *The Limits to Growth* had admitted that information essential to decision was 'fragmentary, contradictory and in some cases unavailable'. This state of affairs, he declared, was the surest way to ruin:

> For more than a thousand years, the predicament of man has been talked about and prayed about in this place. Like those who came here before us, I believe that most of us accept the paramount values embodied in the Pauline virtues of faith, hope and charity. But we cannot but recall that neither the Christian religion nor science offers the expectation that man will flourish in perpetuity upon earth. To the early Christians the apocalypse seemed close. To those of us having some acquaintance with palaeontology, the study of ancient life, the fact that a greater number of species have become extinct than have survived is warning enough. Some of them have vanished abruptly from the record after a great population explosion.[9]

He said that, given accurate knowledge, there remained solid grounds for hope about the future of man and his fellow creatures. But our immediate and paramount need is to advance the environmental and social sciences to the point at which we have convincing data to work with. These scientific objectives have far more than academic interest and make, perhaps, the most urgent claim of all upon our allocation of funds and expertise.

Yet – and this is what scares me most – there seems to be positive resistance on the part of governments and the captains of industry against the advancement of this kind of research. Are they actually afraid of what the findings might be? And dare we allow such fear to put us all in infinitely greater jeopardy? The Australian biologist, Professor Charles Birch, has told how he tried to get started a project on 'The Future of Australia' with the deliberate idea of working out just what the continent's carrying capacity should be. But the proposal foundered, he says, because some Australian economists said that if you want to prosper you must grow, and so there is no point in discussing a halt to growth.

17

'I do not believe that,' commented Birch, 'and fortunately there are some economists who do not believe it either.'

Was it the same studied indifference of vested interests which ensured that the Third UN Conference on Trade and Development in 1972 was a match between 'second elevens'? Why did those rich countries which have a Ministry of Development send only a few trade experts instead of the responsible minister? Why were so many of the seats filled with diplomats? Why did the choice of diplomats and the tactics of the meeting seem to be designed to ensure that the resolutions that were passed on the stabilization of prices and wider sales opportunities for the developing countries need never be implemented?

A possible answer to those questions appeared in a newspaper advertisement on the Sunday on which I started to write this chapter. It was dominated by the head and shoulders of an attractively ordinary young blonde, obviously purring like a cat. The captions, above and below, read:

*You Self-indulgent, Tight fisted,*
*Modern Living, Comfort Lover You . . .*

|  |  |
|---|---|
| **Don't you really** | **Love** unashamed luxury<br>**Hate** parting with your hard-earned money<br>**Love** the good things you work for<br>**Hate** being cold or inconvenienced |

*Why don't you fall in love with the things you really enjoy?*

I regret that the paper did not set this masterpiece alongside an advertisement for Oxfam or Christian Aid. I shall have more to say in a later chapter about the relentless pressures towards consumption under which the citizens of the industrialized countries have to live. The point I want to make here is that the so-called growth economy which our two main political parties take for granted, and which so many economists and industrialists regard as sacrosanct, *is maintained by creating discontent in the rich countries and inescapable poverty in the poor countries.*

I sometimes wonder why the big firms spend so much on advertising consumer goods when all they need to do is to keep up the dull, faceless routine of the factories and the standardized grey cement of the workers' apartment blocks. For, as a *Times* leader pointed out in April 1974, 'It is boredom, not exercise, that creates our appetite.' Eli Chinoy's careful study of automobile workers in the United States shows that the only visible way left for them to acquire a sense of identity and value among their fellows is by acquiring material possessions. New living-room furniture, a washing machine and colour television are the only available confirmation that one is getting ahead. And James Weaver, the American economist, shows up the inner hollowness of the whole structure of growth economy in the simple statement: 'If all of us decided that our homes were adequate, our cars satisfactory, our clothing sufficient, our present sort of economics would collapse tomorrow. For it is built on the assumption that man's wants are insatiable.'

### What matters is now

In its review of *Thinking About the Future*, *The Times Literary Supplement* concluded with these words: 'The MIT model which underlies *The Limits to Growth* can be regarded as dead. But the issues it raises are very much alive.' It seems to me that no responsible person can duck out of that conclusion. E. F. Schumacher has been one of the most stringent critics in Britain of *The Limits to Growth*, mainly on the grounds that it deals with the problems in over-all global terms instead of locating them in areas of particular concentration. As a Christian, he also contends that man, a child of God, is *designed* for growth. He is endowed with great gifts which he is called upon to use. And he goes on:

> It is perfectly obvious that there is no means whatsoever at our disposal to stop either the growth of world capital or of world population. What we can do, however, is to fight the growth of what is unsound and promote the growth of what is sound.[10]

He then proceeds to diagnose as centres of unsound growth the rich countries, taking the USA as a leading example. That country alone, containing only 5·6% of the world's population, has been consuming 42% of the world's output of aluminium, 33% of its copper, 44% of the world's coal, 33% of its petroleum and 63% of its natural gas. And all of these are non-renewable resources. Schumacher's comment is deadly.

> It is obvious that the world cannot afford the USA. Nor can it afford Western Europe or Japan. In fact we might come to the conclusion that the earth cannot afford the 'Modern World'. It requires too much and accomplishes too little. It is too uneconomic. Think of it: one American drawing on resources that would sustain 50 Indians! The earth cannot afford, say, 15% of its inhabitants – the rich who are using all the marvellous achievements of science and technology – to indulge in a crude, materialistic way of life which ravages the earth. The poor don't do much damage; the modest people don't do much damage. Virtually all the damage is done by, say, 15%. It is obvious, therefore, that the Club of Rome exercise, which lumps all people together into a 'world population' and also lumps all production and all consumption together, as if everything were much of a muchness, far from clarifying the tense situation, obscures it. *The problem passengers on Space-ship Earth are the first-class passengers and no one else.*[1]

The heated argument of the doom debate will go on, no doubt, for a long time. I am not qualified to join issue over this or that prognosis of the world's sickness; I am more interested in diagnosis of its present state of health. I have a deep fear that those who might have the skill to give us accurate predictions will not be allowed to do so until it is too late. But a disciple of Christ should be the last person to put aside his share of responsibility for the future with the shrug of despair. As John Poulton has put it:

> Man's future is upon him. Christians will be heard speaking of God most plainly when they are seen to cope with Future Shock as if there is One in control, the Lord of all change, the Lord always coming towards them from that Future.[12]

That faith does not equip us with the skill to measure and predict. We can only clamour through the corridors of power that the experts be aided to do that adequately for the survival of our race. But in the meantime what everyone of us can do is to forgo the lethal folly of our ways and then to throw our whole weight into a sustained campaign against the attitudes of our affluent society and all those who deliberately seek to engender them in us. For, whatever the ins and outs of the doom debate, the message that comes through is clear and simple enough for action. It is intolerable to maintain the ever-rising standards of the few upon the poverty of the many. Any attempt to raise all to parity with the rich will destroy our world. The rich – ourselves – must learn to be content with less. That means that as import prices go up, wages, salaries, dividends, rents and tariffs do not, and we find humane ways of spreading the loss and finding new avenues of employment.

Such a change will certainly not be disastrous for our health nor for our peace of mind. If you doubt that, find out which are the countries with the highest incidence of cancer, thrombosis, back injury, neurosis and suicide. I am not against the good things of life, and I covet for all mankind a level of comfort and security that will make possible the fullest realization of our powers and our mutual enrichment. But those ideals are at the very opposite end of the moral spectrum from the excess which marks our Western way of life, however similar the two may seem to be on the surface. Excess means disproportion; and disproportion can never be a recipe for survival. Excess is the subject of this book and the enemy which I shall try to invite you to fight year in and year out. It confronts us in our rich countries whichever aspect of our situation we look at – our consumption of food and our accumulation of goods, our wage claims and price rises, our waste and pollution, the concentration and congestion of our cities, our destruction of living creatures and our plunder of fuels and minerals, our expenditure on armaments and the wanton disproportion of the way we use them – *excess* is the word that comes continually to mind: ruthless, unbridled, unthinking excess. We are being made to expect too much. We are taking too much. We are scrapping too much. We are paying, and compelling others to pay, far too high a price.

21

# 2

## Spoilt Children

'If it had grown up,' she said to herself, 'it would have made a dreadfully ugly child: but it makes rather a handsome pig, I think.' And she began thinking over other children she knew, who might do very well as pigs . . .

*Alice's Adventures in Wonderland*

### Real men have four wheels

I know that I have to leave the economic interpretation of our behaviour to the conflicting opinions of the experts. We need no experts, however, to point out the state of mind, the psychological attitudes, which this behaviour betrays. It is the state of mind of a spoilt child, petulantly greedy and ready to kick to bits anything that frustrates its will. That is what I see in the various examples I want to touch on in this chapter.

Undeterred by 50,000 motoring deaths per year, the output of automobiles in the USA has recently been growing twice as rapidly as the population. There is now virtually one car for every second citizen – man, woman or child. In Britain, car-owners are still in the minority. In central London, surprisingly, 80% of people use public transport to get around to work or to the shops, 10% walk and only 10% use their own cars and clog the system. It is, in fact, a shock to realize how much congestion, fumes and noise can be imposed upon the inner city by only 10% of the people there; the effect of raising that number to only 20% would be quite intolerable. Yet in every British city now this minority of private car commuters seems to enjoy the right of inflicting an almost unlimited nuisance on the majority.

Together with the generation of electricity, private cars account for most of our air pollution. Yet, instead of restricting the use of private transport in the centre of our great cities – a common-sense reform which most car-owners I have talked to would secretly applaud – a vast acreage of precious space is devoured by the never-ending programme of road widening. At the present time in the United States a million acres a year are lost from agriculture to transport systems and the unplanned urban sprawl which springs from them; that is, two acres every minute. So much for our concern for mankind's food supply! City planners do not decide how much road space is compatible with good urban life and the convenience of the residents. They allow the private car to dictate to them. They argue that, at whatever cost, road space must be provided to accommodate whatever number of private cars are likely to demand it in the foreseeable future. The car-owner, and even more the car-manufacturer, is the sole arbiter in this matter. And this is extraordinary, when one considers the following equation, which has been endorsed by many studies of what happens when a length of roadway in the city is, for one reason or another, thrown out of use for a few days. Adapt the city to suit the car and the results are atrocious; adapt the use of the car to the needs of the city and almost no one is inconvenienced.

What causes the trouble is not car-ownership but its totally indiscriminate use. Most of the 10% of those commuting by car into central London drive alone. The chairman of the London Transport Executive stated in 1973 that if 700 people want to come into London, they fill one train, or fourteen buses, or 500 cars. At about that time a photograph appeared in *The Observer* showing a one-way street in central London choked with cars – 69 of them in about 200 yards. Yet one bus could have carried all the people who were in those cars and would virtually have had the street to itself. If cars were banned in the inner city, the speed of public transport could increase so dramatically that travellers would enjoy a cut of about 70% off the time of their journeys across the city and at a much lower price. But, as things are, private car congestion has disrupted the bus system, so that now, absurdly, a journey costs more by public transport than by private car.

Robert Priestley, writing in an *Observer Colour Magazine* later that year, had this to say:

> The door-to-door motorized comfort of those who have taken to driving themselves (or being driven by company car) to work is purchased at the price of leaving the cost and increasing discomfort and frustration of an indispensable but under-subscribed public transport system to be borne by those least able to afford and endure it – the young, the old and the poor. It is the poor, too, who suffer and will increasingly suffer (by way of increasing rent and homelessness) as land gets scarcer and dearer.

If any large city in Britain made it illegal to bring any private vehicle within the circle of a ring-road along which, at intervals, enough multi-storey garages were provided both for those who approached the city by car and for car owners living in the city, and if from those points a comprehensive network was provided by mini-buses, travelling as swiftly as the uncongested roads would then allow, everyone's experience of the city would become very much more civilized. Vans and lorries should normally be compelled to do all their collecting and delivering by night, using only certain roads of access to the warehouses, factories, markets and shops. Certainly this would entail the expense of night staff; but this would to a considerable extent be offset by reduction of rates in respect of traffic control and the upkeep and widening of roads.

The private car, used as a commuter vehicle, is an important factor in the uncontrolled, unplanned development of our monstrous modern conurbations. No authority can design a coherent city, with properly related areas for residents, trade, business, industry and recreation, with 'lungs' of open space and with a firmly drawn outer limit, as long as this unrestrained private transport makes possible the proliferation of dormitory suburbs to an unlimited distance from the city centre.

There is nothing inevitable about this. Many city-planners, and many representatives of motoring interests are convinced that a drastic limit must be imposed on the use of private cars in the centre of our cities, for the sake of the quality of urban life. Alisdaer Aird, for example, editor of *Motoring Which*, who drives his car daily from Tonbridge to Charing Cross has gone on record with this confession:

> I really need someone to take the decision out of my hands. If the Greater London Council stopped private cars going into the centre of town, I would be quite grateful to them.

Yet there seems very little chance that any city council can withstand the vested interests of a national motor industry or the international oil companies. For once it finds itself in a situation of competition, big business seems to find it impossible to settle for less than the whole cake. The various industries are not out to create wealth, but simply to create their *own* wealth.

In the eighteenth century, for example, Britain's incomparable network of canals, developed by such engineering geniuses as James Brindley and Thomas Telford, was the nerve system of the industrial revolution. Birmingham has more miles of canal than Venice. Tunnelled through the hills, lifted on elegant aqueducts above the rivers or on broad embankments over the dry valleys, curving with the contours of the landscape, these waterways were things of great beauty as well as usefulness. One fully loaded barge today carries the equivalent of five lorries. But then came the railways, and they saw the canals as rivals. In Europe the two systems were seen to be complementary and today the canals of France, Germany, Austria and the Low Countries offer a viable alternative to rail and road for heavy industrial loads. In 1969 237 million tons was waterborne in Holland alone, but less than 7 million in Britain. What happened? The nineteenth-century rail companies in Britain and in the USA were allowed systematically to buy up the canals, then starve them of trade and neglect their maintenance, until there was no choice but to close them down. A much needed and a very beautiful asset was destroyed for the sake of a new interest that could neither accept limits nor brook rivals. That is what I mean by the mentality of a spoilt child. And now, as a fantastic nemesis of repeated waste, it is the turn of Britain's marvellous railway network to be sacrificed to the jealousy of the next usurper – road transport. Every few years larger regions of Britain are made virtually inaccessible to any but car owners or long-distance juggernauts. The abandonment of thousands of miles of track, with its tunnels, embankments, viaducts and shunting yards, is a monumental price to pay for the monopoly of a nation's transport. But we are no longer living in an integrated society where the profit or loss of the *whole* is taken into account and where it is still conceivable to take no for an answer; we are dealing with communal emotions and instincts which, having been fostered deliberately over many decades, are now running amock. The private car, and even, to a lesser extent, the juggernaut lorry, has been turned into a highly charged symbol of aggressive independence. The motor industry is not selling cars, it is selling power, virility, status and self-assertion.

The *New Yorker* wrily remarked some years ago that there were still some people in America who see a motor car primarily as a mode of transportation, but that you would never infer that from a study of the sales talk. Vance Packard picked a highly-coloured bunch from the advertisements fifteen years ago.

Plymouth quoted a happy family, standing before their long, long car, as disclosing proudly, 'We are not wealthy . . . we just look it!' Dodge, in one of its radio commercials, depicted an admiring man exclaiming excitedly to a Dodge owner: 'Boy, you must be rich to own a car as big as this!' . . . Ford depicted an actress pointing to the Ford's enormous tail lights, and explained that they 'let the people behind you know you are ahead of them!' Edsel, in picturing across two pages of colour a family driving up to a $60,000 or $70,000 house, stated: 'They'll know you've *arrived* when you drive up in an Edsel.'[1]

As flamboyant length and thrusting angles became one of the essentials of car design, some cities had to take down their parking meters and plant them further apart. It has been observed also that a remarkable number of car-owners, when they return from work, leave their vehicles at the kerb side in front of their home, and only after dark, if at all, drive them to the lock-up or to their own garage; for their primary function is to be seen. The obvious sexual symbolism of the car and its powers of acceleration have been exploited in the same way; it is not by chance that the Motor Show was the first industrial shop-window to adorn its goods with live girls in, or even out of, bikinis! To curtail the use of the private car is to threaten a kind of castration. So the claims of the owner driver are supported with a ruthless disregard of other interests and of ultimate costs.

That is what I mean by excess. I am not concerned with numbers but with disproportion. I am not worried by the many but by the mania.

### The waste-mongers

But, of course, not all the cars on the road are travelling any more. With 50 million of them darting like minnows across the darkening surface of the United States, the pressure is on to persuade all the owners to turn in their present models. So year by year 7 million are junked – 70,000 of them abandoned in the streets of New York alone. The old adage, 'Waste not, want not', is endorsed by the champions of growth as a principle in an entirely negative sense. Those who won't waste don't want: since we want them to want, we must make them waste. So along with 7 million discarded cars in the States go 48 billion metal cans, 26 billion bottles and 65 billion metal bottle caps. The steel in the vehicles is recycled in a desultory way, but no one seems interested in bottles. For the same reason, the junk rooms and the cellars and the bottom shelves of larders in most of the homes of Britain are overflowing with glass jars and bottles which no firm will take back, with the honourable exception of the milk retailers. And even they are threatening plastic now.

No one wants plastic back. It is so cheap to make and costs so much to use again, or to destroy. Its indestructability, in fact, is its greatest horror. A holiday month in the Shetlands in 1973 was full of the atmosphere of doomed resignation as the day of the oil-rigs drew near. But already the white sands and pastel-shaded rocks of those remote shores were fouled with a deposit of plastic sheeting and containers of all shapes and sizes. This was not the litter of tourists nor of the vanguard of the oil companies' Irish labourers; it had come in on the tides from the shipping of the North Sea. It was simply *homo affluens* marking his triumphal path along the sea lanes and highways of the world with a more enduring substance than all the stones of Ozymandias.

Any concentrated population is bound to present a problem of waste disposal. Industry has to deal somehow with its own effluents. But the spoilt child of the Western nursery scatters his cast-offs and his broken plastic toys about the room, assuming that his two nursemaids, air and water, will go on clearing up the mess as they always have. He needs to learn, and learn quickly, that air and water do not belong to him alone, and that their services are *not* free. Both industry and the private citizen must be taught the common courtesy of clearing up after themselves, by bearing full financial responsibility for the thorough disposal or recycling of their wastes, instead of passing them on to their unfortunate neighbours. For today the tides of trade and tourism are ubiquitous, and Western enterprise is piling the same mountains of garbage on the markets of the Third World. What falls from the rich man's table is not crumbs but poisons and plastics.

Technology can deal with this problem of disposal if producers and consumers are compelled to pay for the solution by, for example, accepting a tax on cans and bottles that cannot be easily recycled, and installing, as a few cities have done, plant that burns garbage to generate electricity and returns the city's waste to the land in the form of compost. But the spoilt child wants too much for too little. The individual consumer doesn't want to include in the price of his purchases the real cost of disposing of the left-overs; and firms refuse to bear the cost of recycling or treating

28

their waste product, unless they are given tax relief. Private profit matters more than public environment.

The effect of deliberately fostering this throw-away mentality is incalculable. It very quickly seeps back into the places where it has been generated – the industries and business houses themselves. The con-men fall for their own conning. Waste becomes endemic even in the processes that are supposed to be making the wealth. A flagrant example of this is the energy industry. Just as the railways indulged in the gigantic throw-away of an efficient canal-system, and were themselves, in turn, thrown away by the British road-transport interests, the same one-track mindedness sets the electrical power industry against the coal-gas industry and both against the fuel-oil industry. This absurd charade of competition makes it possible for the electricity generating industry, while striving to get one half per cent extra efficiency out of the turbines and heat exchangers, blandly to dump the energy of 75% of the fuel it has consumed. But the Central Electricity Generating Board has only one purpose – to produce electricity. It is not interested in what happens to all the steam it produces, which, as has been proved in Germany and Sweden, is a far more economical form of home-heating, releasing electricity for the higher thermal needs for which it is more appropriate. But no; the master-minds of Growth are by now themselves infected with the throw-away mentality they have done so much to spread abroad. At the end of the day, to cultivate the habit of wastefulness will always prove wasteful.

We all bemoan from time to time the passing of the 'little man on the corner' who could put a new handle on an old suitcase, repair an electric fire or re-cane a chair; or, at moments of despair, we remember that ever-resourceful neighbour who could always produce from the back of a drawer gluepot or soldering iron or carpet needle and an offer of help that never made one's helplessness too obvious. Now it is not only their kind that has departed but, alas, their values also. Rapid turnover is the trend for our ideas, our commitments, our jobs, our local loyalties, our friendships and even our marriages. Of course this does not all derive from the 'make but never mend' philosophy of growth economy. But there are connections of a kind. Perhaps all these developments, including our blind worship of growth, are symptoms of a second-degree materialism, when we are 'hooked' not on things but on change. It is the malaise to which Alvin Toffler gave the not very enlightening name of Future Shock.

## The global gardyloo

God forgive us if ever again we turn up supercilious white noses at the open drains of Asian and African cities, or snigger when we read again of that old cry from the upper windows of Edinburgh's mediaeval streets – Gardyloo! – which, as they learned from the euphemistic French of the palace (beware of the water!), was the proper warning that the household slops were about to be flung out. For the world has had to wait until the arrival of scientific, technological man to see its rivers, seas and atmosphere, not only treated as drains and sewers, but made to receive an ever-growing load of poisonous chemicals and gases, thermal and radio-active waste, harmful metallic substances, crude oil leaks, fertilizer and detergent run-off, inadequately treated sewage, and non-soluble containers. In his report *Polluting Britain*, Jeremy Bugler gave a horrifying account of the fouling of the river Mersey.

> Every day forty-five factories, refineries and industrial plants release fifty-two million gallons of trade effluent into the estuary, much of it in a poorer condition than would be permitted for a river discharge. It is also a massive unflushed lavatory.[2]

We are by now familiar with the marvellous interdependence of life systems on which our very survival depends. I have been told that in the vineyards of California they plant small patches of blackberries at intervals to prevent the spread of the grape leafhopper which can do enormous damage. It appears that the blackberries have a different leafhopper of their own, and parasites that build up on the blackberry leafhopper spread to the vines and make havoc of the grape leafhoppers. Without the

30

blackberries there are not enough parasites to keep the grape leafhoppers controlled. Diversity is one of nature's oldest stratagems. That is why the great English ecologist, Charles Elton, tried so hard to persuade farmers to maintain hedgerows between the fields because their profusion of different species of plants offered a natural reserve for an enormous variety of small predator birds, reptiles, insects and parasites, most of which help to keep down pests or to assist pollination in the fields. But with all the ruthlessness of the single-track mind, farmers have grasped at the new mechanized hedge-cutters which rip out many species of flora, so that today it is hard to find primroses on any of the banks in the Isle of Wight. And as if that were not enough, they have smothered the poor, denuded hedgerows with fertilizers and pesticides.

I have spoken in a very English manner of hedgerows and fields; but we have to think in terms of forests and vast wheatlands. In 1962 the world market needed 1,000 million cubic metres of wood. By 1975 it is reckoned that this figure will have doubled. But it is the trees that protect the soil and regulate the flow of water. The great flood in Florence in 1966 was primarily due to unrestrained deforestation in the Etruscan Apennines.

So then the unprotected soil and the pesticides and fertilizers are sluiced down into the rivers and the seas to join the industrial wastes and the detergents and the sewage and the garbage. All the organic matter, with the phosphates and nitrates of the fertilizers, gives the tiny water algae one glorious moment of excess all their own; but, like all excess, it kills them off. As the layer of microscopic bodies thickens, light for their photosynthesis cannot penetrate, and they die, producing more organic matter which, in process of decomposition by bacteria, uses up the oxygen from the water. At that point the river or lake dies, in so far as its purifying and life-sustaining capacity is concerned. Some years ago that had started to happen to the Thames until stringent measures were imposed upon industries in its catchment area. It has happened to Lake Erie; it is happening to the Parramatta river in Australia. The Cleveland river is so choked with oil and debris it is classified as a 'fire hazard'. In the summer of 1969 40 million fish suddenly died of poisoning in the Rhine. A sportsman trying to swim the length of the Lake of Geneva was forced to give up halfway by the gases rising from the surface. Great numbers of people in recent years have contracted hepatitis on Rome's sea-bathing beaches; the less fortunate fishermen around the southern shores of Japan are more likely to get what is called the 'Mad Hatter's Disease' from mercury poisoning.

The air, like the water which, as I have said before, man has always expected, like a nursemaid, to clear up his mess, has a strictly limited power of absorption. It cannot cope with the accumulations of toxic gases and particles in the quantities in which we now release them. Says Bugler:

> Manufacturers employing the new technologies have not paid all their bills. They have treated the air and landscape as 'free goods'. While they have met such internal costs as raw materials and the labour bill, they have left to society to pay the costs of pollution. This externalizing of costs, this public subsidy of (usually) private industry has produced what the American biologist Garrett Hardin has called 'the tragedy of the commons' – air, land and water being a kind of unfenced common.[3]

### Anything goes

If this devastation of the delicate balance of nature has been carried on largely through ignorance, one might hope that the new knowledge would bring new sense. Unhappily, however, we are not dealing with sense, but with that which is insensate. For a long time men have known well enough what the score was if they continued unchecked in the modern methods of whaling. It could not escape their notice that, since 1945, more and more whales have been killed to produce less and less oil. The simple reason for this was that all the larger whales had been extermi-nated. First this so-called industry killed off the biggest whales, the blues, which are now very rare indeed. (It is now estimated that in only 30 years the total blue whale population of the world has dropped from 100,000 to 1,000 or less.) Then, as those stocks gave out, the industry turned to the great fin whales; as they reached extermination point the whalers transferred their attentions to the much smaller sizes. And now the last species, the sperm, is being hunted without restraint. In a scientific age one would have thought that the most elementary principles of husbandry would have dictated limits, and that the governments of the world would have found ways of enforcement, even on the high seas. We managed it with the elephant when we were the big-game hunters and wanted to corner the market in ivory.

To hunt any species to the point of extinction shows a kind of madness, for not only does that particular industry kill itself, but a part of the richness of creation has been irreparably destroyed. And for what? To a considerable extent, the whales are slaughtered today to feed Western man's domestic pets.

Properly controlled, the world's fisheries might be counted upon to produce three times as much protein food as they do at present, without diminishing the supply. But our greedy, unrestrained pillage of the seas is threatening to bring one species after another to extinction. This may seem difficult to believe when we think of the vast expanse and depth of the oceans. We have grown up with the belief that there are plenty of other fish in the sea! But only 5% of them all live in the deep oceans. 95% of the food from the sea must come from coastal waters; and these are the ones where fishing is already destructively intensive, and also where pollution does most damage. The Australian biologist, Charles Birch, speaking at a symposium on 'The Consequences of World Population Growth' in Australia in August 1972, said:

Since 1950 world fish yields increased each year but this increase came to an abrupt halt in 1969; there was a decline of 2%. Six major world fish stocks have declined markedly in the past 25 years, and show no sign of recovery, they include the East Asian sardine, the Northwest Pacific salmon and the Atlanto-Scandinavian herring. In the early stages of fishing supply is virtually unlimited. Harvesting makes little or no dent in the supply. Soon techniques improve and they overtake replacement rates of the stocks. As stocks fall competition to get more is increased while the getting is good. The rate of fishing efficiency increases, until a point arises when improved fishing technology coincides with the near extinction of the species.[4]

There are those who would reply: What would you have the human creature do when he is faced with world-wide starvation? It is a fair question; but one suspects those who ask it, knowing, as I have said, that Peru's anchovy crop does not go to feed the slum-dwellers of Lima but to the intensive broiler houses and veal-pens of the industrialized countries. Whales have not, for the most part, been hunted mainly for their meat, but for the ambergris of our expensive perfumes, for the whalebone (yes even now!) for the corset industry, for the manufacture of pet-foods and for the oil which was sought, originally, for its value in the manufacture of nitro-glycerine and only latterly for processed foods. There's not much for the world's poor in that list. No; what fires the harpoons is not need, but greed. Theodore Roszak has written:

> Those who anguish over a starving mankind on the easy assumption that there just is not enough land and resources to feed the hungry, might do well to pay a special kind of visit to their local supermarket. Not to shop, but to observe and to meditate on what they see before them and had always taken for granted. How much of the world's land and labor was wasted producing the tobacco, the coffee, the tea, the refined cane sugars, the polished rice, the ice-creams, the candies, the cookies, the soft drinks, the thousand and one non-nutritional luxuries one finds there? The grains that became liquor, the fruits and vegetables that lost all their food value going into cans and jars full of syrups and condiments, the potatoes and corn that became various kinds of chips, crackles, crunchies and yum-yums, the cereals that became breakfast novelties less nourishing (as a matter of scientific fact) than the boxes they are packed in, the wheat that became white breads and pastry flours ... How many forests perished to package these non-foods? How many resources went into transporting and processing them? (And the less nutrition, the more processing.) How much skilled energy went into advertising and merchandising them? There they stand in our markets, row upon row, aisle upon aisle of nutritional zero, gaily boxed and packed, and costing those fancy prices we then gripe about as the high cost of living.[5]

34

Even that does not tell the full price that is paid. We should need to ask the battery hens, the anaemic veal-calves and other creatures condemned to live their lives in semi-darkness or artificial light, unable to walk or turn, with environmental disease kept at bay only by the addition of pharmaceutical drugs and tranquillizers to their diet.

Many farmers, thank God, are angry at the pressures being put upon them to conform. In Wales a number of them fired shots at the home of a colleague for setting up an intensive unit. A former agricultural correspondent to the *Daily Mail* wrote more than a decade ago:

> Rightly or wrongly, I hate the idea of keeping hens in those wire chests of drawers they call batteries. I think it is cruel and also that it produces an inferior article of food. It's no good telling me that they wouldn't thrive if they were unhappy. The time when I really put on weight was when I sat in trenches for a year, dirty, wet, frightened and miserable.[6]

When we hear some news-item about the agricultural policies of the European Economic Community we must erase from our memories the fair fields of France or contented cattle in a Dutch landscape and think instead of ministries determined to put on the pressure to set up larger and more intensive units. Such a unit is to all intents and purposes a factory, applying production-line methods to the rearing of birds or animals which, in the words of Ruth Harrison, 'have put evolution into reverse and depressed the animal back towards the plant stage in an effort to turn it into an efficient food-into-flesh converting machine'.[6] Patrick Goldring, in his book *The Broiler House Society*, has described the scene inside one of the vast huts where the birds we meet only as pallid frosty plastic lumps on the poultry counter, have actually lived and moved (a little) and had their brief being:

> Barely visible in a dim red light, are several thousand chickens crowded wing to wing and jostling around the food hoppers and water bowls spaced at intervals down the gloomy length of the shed. There is underfloor electric heating. Food and water are provided automatically. The ventilator extracts some of the smell, disinfectant is sprayed

regularly and the wood shavings on the floor are turned over occasionally to cover the droppings. Chicks come here from the hatcheries one day old and spend their entire lives – a precisely calculated sixty days – inside the broiler house. Until the day they die they never see the sun, never feel the wind or the rain, never set foot on honest earth.[7]

Another expert, a working veterinary surgeon, has said that after examining a great many broiler-house birds and battery layers, he would judge that they show evident signs of extreme stress and, quite early on in the experience, lose their minds. Perhaps this is just as well, for when their time comes the birds are taken in enormous numbers to the slaughter house and shackled by their legs to the conveyor belt. As this moves slowly towards the slaughter man the birds may hang for some time before they are killed, and this concentrates the blood in their heads so that they bleed more rapidly when their throats are finally cut. More packing stations are beginning to instal stunners to knock the birds out before they reach the slaughter man, but this is by no means universal. I can only tell the rest of the story by quoting from Ruth Harrison's *Animal Machines*.

> They then flap their blood out in a 'bleeding tunnel' at the other end of which is a scalding tank. It is estimated that of the birds which have their throats cut in full consciousness, two out of every five go into the scalding tank alive. A leading veterinary surgeon has stated that in his opinion jugular severance without prior stunning is grossly inhumane.[8]

I have not recounted this in such detail in order to harrow readers. And I shall not attempt to describe the lamb-cages, the unicars for cows nor the sweat boxes for pigs. It is easy to work up sentiment on behalf of the animals; but we have to admit there is a wide area of doubt about the quality of animal suffering. We are on perfectly sure ground, however, when we weigh up what we are doing to *ourselves* when we allow livestock to be treated in this way. This is quite different from the bullying cruelty of little boys stoning a cat or the blind rage of a peasant thrashing his mule. Those are fully human actions, albeit out of control; but this is non-human, though those who cause these things to be done, at whatever remove along the chain of command and re-sponsibility, are coolly in control of themselves. Except at one point. The point at which someone knows no control, cannot take no for an answer: the point of excess.

It is not an excess of the need for food. The protein-rich linseed oil from India, like the fishmeal from Peru, ended up in that broiler house. Together with goodness-knows-what admixtures of vaccines, hormones, growth regulators and tranquillizers they went to make that insipid or sometimes fishy poultry flesh that awaits us on the counter. It may make us fatter and give more work to the slimming industry; but whether, with its peculiar pharmaceutical history, it will make us healthier is more doubtful. And in any case by now we are over-producing milk, chickens and eggs. Why, else, the advertising campaigns but to boost up demand to meet the output? Eggs are going into paint, cosmetics and shampoos as well as stomachs. So the excess that brought us to this point was not an excess of need.

Nor was it of greed – not physical greed. In the places where the gourmets gather and honest gluttony lives on they do not order their meat and poultry from the large intensive units. No; the excess is of those who by conviction or complicity say that what a business exists for is to make wealth and that it cannot go on doing so unless it makes more.

It is with some relief that I turn to a further example of this peculiar deadly madness of our days, though the final example which lies beyond it is the most terrifying of them all. Shakespeare knew how to bring on the clown just before the climax of the tragedy, and the clown in this case is called Concorde – though that rather more successful family of tumblers, the Apollos, would have served my purpose as well. This particular turn is called 'Money No Object' and there are two ways of presenting it. One was a neat little graph, about two inches square, which accompanied an article in one of the Sunday papers – I forget which, having clipped out the graph for its own sake. The vertical lines from left to right indicate the years 1963–1972. The horizontal gradations show successive estimations of the cost, each step representing £100 million, ten stages from zero to £1,000 million. And then there is a broad straight diagonal running from the second lowest square on the left to the highest possible square on the right. No exponential curves – a child might have done it, or a clown. It was the neatest punch-line I have seen for a long while. The other way of presenting this comic turn is Bernard Levin's:

> The sheer *impudence* of the Concorde project is what I find most striking about it. Year after year, ministers have announced that the cost will, after all, be several hundred million pounds higher than the previous estimate; after a bit, they even abandoned the old trick of slipping in the news at the end of the session in a written answer. Year after year, long after it had become apparent it could never, even on the most absurdly optimistic forecast of sales, make a profit or even come within hundreds of millions of pounds of breaking even, the pretence was kept up that this albatross-shaped white elephant was going to make Britain's national fortune.[9]

Of course, what keeps us all so fascinated by this clowns routine is that there is always a chance that Concorde may have the last laugh.

But I, for one, shan't join in. For halfway through his comical turn I saw his mask slip. And behind the pierrot's face I saw the obsessed, somnambulistic stare of Vietnam. That is the place-name by which we know it now, though by the time this book is published it may go by another. But it will be the same thing, the spirit that cannot take no for an answer and knows no bounds, because it is inherently out of bounds. Perhaps I am talking about the Devil, but I hesitate to say so because we always blame him for everything. So perhaps I am still only talking about a spoilt child. In any case the word 'Vietnamization' describes not what President Nixon meant, but something that was happening to human beings that was able to carry them coolly, doggedly, fanatically to the point where there was nothing, literally nothing, they would not choose to destroy rather than have their will frustrated. In their different ways the powers on both sides of the conflict were engulfed in the same obsession. More than a million combatants were killed and perhaps more than a million civilians too. Do the figures matter any more? We saw it in our own drawing-rooms, as no war has ever been seen before, but could we go on feeling it any more? More than 6 million acres of valuable forest trees and food crops were deliberately defoliated with chemicals, 90,000 tons of them. Bulldozers scraped fertile top soil from almost as large an area again and the face of the country was pocked with 26 million bomb craters, reducing it indiscriminately to a moon landscape. When all is paid, the eventual cost to America is currently estimated at £125 billion. It is beside the point to ask what this will achieve or what it was for. We are not dealing with that kind of rationality. If we were, the continued use of the new kinds of weapons against human flesh and blood would have been unthinkable. If we were, the astronomical waste of our world's expenditure on armaments would appear as an unbelievable madness. But we are dealing with a self will and a fear that are so enraged and so totally out of control that they could, in the last resort, unleash the nuclear holocaust rather than cry 'Enough!'

But Vietnamization is not something that happens 'over there'. And I realize I have allowed the last few pages to run away with me and have got the tone all wrong for my purposes. For Vietnamization is only the darker face of excess, the inconsolable petulance of the spoilt child. It is all around us today. It even goes by the name of 'having fun'. As Erich Fromm says:

> Having fun lies in the satisfaction of consuming and 'taking in' com-modities, sights, food, drinks, cigarettes, people, lectures, books, movies – all are consumed, swallowed. The world is one great object for our appetite, a big apple, a big bottle, a big breast; we are the suck-lers, the eternally expectant ones, the hopeful ones – and the eternally disappointed ones. Our character is geared to exchange and to receive, to barter and to consume; everything, spiritual as well as material objects, becomes an object of exchange and of consumption.[10]

It seems we never got out of the nursery.

# 3

## The Theology of Enough

'. . . the patriotic Archbishop of Canterbury, found it advisable –
'Found *what*?' said the Duck.
'Found *it*,' the Mouse replied rather crossly: 'of course you know
what "it" means.'
'I know what "it" means well enough, when *I* find a thing,' said
the Duck: 'it's generally a frog or a worm. The question is, what did
the archbishop find?'

*Alice's Adventures in Wonderland*

### The dream of shalom

Let me repeat that I am not arguing about the future, but about
the present. If I have touched on our society's reluctance to impose the most obvious restrictions on the flow of private transport
to our inner cities, or its tacit collusion with brutalizing methods
of intensive farming, or its frenetic output of short-lived, throw-
away products, or the 'money's no object' approach to the costing
of our more flamboyant enterprises, or the spiralling expectations
we call a rising standard of living, my object is not to calculate
where we shall be by the end of the century, but to disclose what
manner of civilization we have become and what kind of spirit it
is that possesses and drives us. As I said before, my concern is
diagnosis more than prognosis, and I believe that what is wrong
is not so much what we are doing as the frame of reference
within which we are doing it, or, if you like, not so much our
way of grabbing at things as our way of looking at things. Our

sickness is more like eye disease than heart disease. But don't for a minute imagine that that is less serious, for didn't Jesus say: 'If the eyes are bad, your whole body will be in darkness. If then the only light you have is darkness, the darkness is doubly dark'?

History may have more to teach us than calculations about the future. Diagnosis, after all, is based on previous cases. So I find the economics of ancient Rome significant, because the perspective of history enables me to relate the economics to the whole culture and to the sickness of heart that was already infecting it. A footnote in Paul Johnson's fascinating book, *The Offshore Islanders*, recalls that in the first century AD a pound of gold was the equivalent of 1,000 denarii, the basic silver coin.[1] The silver coinage declined steadily in relation to gold, and in the mid-third century the monetary system disintegrated. In 301 Diocletian attempted to stabilize the currency on the basis of 50,000 denarii to a pound of gold; but a decade later the figure was 120,000. By 324 it had risen to 300,000 and by 337 it was 20 million; in the 350s it was 330 million. The Roman Empire was destroyed by inflation, though this itself was the result of deeper causes.

Again, let me remind you that it is those deeper causes that I am interested in rather than the economic symptoms of them. A culture is an outward expression of the dreams by which men live. 'Any dream will do,' sang Joseph, in the cheerful musical version of the Bible story that was showing in London two years ago. But he was mistaken; the content of the dream makes all the difference. In the Bible it is the Hebrew dream that matters. In practice their two little kingdoms fell far short of the ideal; yet the ideal lived on as a dream, not only in the visions and vituperations of the prophets, but in the value judgments of ordinary people and, no doubt, in a great deal of daily behaviour too. Their dream was summed up in the word *shalom*, something much broader than 'peace': the harmony of a caring community informed at every point by its awareness of God. And in that definition the kernel of *shalom*'s meaning is in the phrase 'at every point'. It speaks of a wholeness that is complete because every aspect and every corner of ordinary life is included. It was a concept deeply rooted in animism. This quotation from *The Biblical Doctrine of Man in Society* by Ernest Wright, for example, might have been taken from any good book on African traditional society.

> The mutual relations of the individual with family, tribe and people are a part of the consitution of the self . . . 'No man is an island'. The individual lives in a web of relations that reach out to other men, and that reach back to those before him and forward to those that live after him. And these relations constitute in a real sense a considerable part of his identity and of his immortality.[2]

What the Hebrews seemed to have perceived with particular vividness and to have articulated most clearly was the fact that this all-embracing inter-relatedness and answerability arose from one primary relationship which God had initiated. All the threads in their network of relationships, their 'bundle of life', seemed to run directly to a single nexus in the hand of God. The *shalom* depended on him. It was the blessing, benediction and benefaction in one, which he had covenanted to give them for ever.

The blessedness of this inter-related, God-related community might be thought of either as wholeness or as harmony. The wholeness was the all-inclusiveness of the framework of reference; the harmony was the reciprocity of all the parts. It meant a dancing kind of inter-relationship, seeking something more free than equality, more generous than equity, the ever-shifting equipoise of a life-system.

Economically and socially this dream of *shalom* found expression in what I call the theology of enough. We shall not find in scripture the blueprint of an economic system relevant to our own day. What we do find is a number of independent enactments, moral judgments and traditions, obviously relating to different periods and cultural backgrounds, all of them utterly different in detail from that which we know today, and yet together revealing a consistent attitude and style diametrically opposed to the excess which I have been describing in the previous two chapters.

## The overweening greed

There are many references in the Old Testament to covetousness and greed, and in more cases than not the Hebrew word which is used means 'desire' or 'longing' which in itself is not bad. One can long for God or for a sight of Jerusalem or for a good meal. That sort of desire becomes sinful only when it is set on wrong or inappropriate things, or when it gets out of proportion. Ordinary covetousness is simply a persistent longing for something that isn't yours. But apart from all this the Hebrews had a word, *betsa*, which is desire of a different sort. It is invariably condemned, and it seems to combine the idea of vaunting ambition and of unjust or fraudulent means. It comes out strongly in Jeremiah's reproachful condemnation of a new king's ostentatious redecoration and enlargement of the palace.

Shame on the man who builds his house by unjust means
and completes its roof-chambers by fraud,
making his countrymen work without payment,
giving them no wage for their labour!
Shame on the man who says, 'I will build a spacious house
     with airy roof-chambers,
set windows in it, panel it with cedar
     and paint it with vermilion'!
If your cedar is more splendid,
     does that prove you a king?
Think of your father: he ate and drank,
dealt justly and fairly, all went well with him.
     He dispensed justice to the lowly and poor;
did not this show he knew me? says the Lord.
But you have no eyes, no thought for anything but gain (*betsa*),
     set only on the innocent blood you can shed,
     on cruel acts of tyranny. (Jeremiah 22.13–17)

In many places the New English Bible fails to bring out the bitter strength of this word *betsa*. It merely speaks about 'the guilt of Israel' in Isaiah 57.17 where the Revised Version says 'the iniquity of his covetousness' and Knox translates 'greedy wrong-doer'. In Exodus 18.21, where Jethro is recommending Moses to

43

delegate part of his authority to deputies, the Revised Version has the phrase 'hating unjust gain' (in many passages *betsa* is something to be hated), but the New English Bible makes it sound like a job-specification for a parish council: 'capable, God-fearing men . . . honest and incorruptible'. For that reason the best way of conveying the meaning of this word is to give it in the context of another longer quotation, this time from Habakkuk 2.9–11. Here again the NEB is weak on this word, failing to convey the strength of repetition in verb and noun in the first line.

> Woe betide you who seek unjust gain for your house,
> to build your nest on a height,
> to save yourself from the grasp of wicked men!
> Your schemes to overthrow mighty nations
>     will bring dishonour to your house
>     and put your own life in jeopardy.
> The very stones will cry out from the wall,
> and from the timbers a beam will answer them.

In both the passages which I have quoted at length there is a vivid imagery of proud arrogance reaching too high and toppling to a fall. It is very close to the Greek idea of *hubris* because the essential fault was one of disproportion. Remembering the ideal of *shalom*, we might say that in Hebrew thought this sin lay in a narrow-minded obsession with one's personal desire and ambition which put on blinkers so that all the beautiful inter-relationships with fellow-men, with the land, with the past and the future, were ignored or forgotten. But you can't join in an intricate square dance wearing blinkers; you lose your sense of the whole and your position in it, and eventually you lose your balance. In the Hebrew mind the sin of excessive covetousness was so evil because it threatened the equipoise of the covenant people.

The later Hebrews' instinctive horror of voracious greed was epitomized in the book of Proverbs:

> The leech has two daughters;
> 'Give', says one and 'give', says the other.
> Three things there are which will never be satisfied,
> four which never say 'Enough!'

The grave and a barren womb,
a land thirsty for water
and fire that never says, 'Enough!' (Proverbs 30.15–16)

Such a spirit was especially deplorable and dangerous when it infected the nation's spiritual leaders.

Israel's watchmen are blind, all of them unaware.
They are all dumb dogs who cannot bark,
stretched on the ground, dreaming, lovers of sleep,
greedy dogs that can never have enough. (Isaiah 56.10–11)

### The virtue of fitting in

Turning to the New Testament we find the same stern veto against grasping excess as we have found in the Mosaic law. In the gospels and epistles a word that is commonly translated 'covetousness', *pleonexia*, does in fact mean 'excess' or 'wanting more and more'. The New English Bible translates it as 'ruthless greed'. It is often linked with sexual lust with which it has so much in common. 'From inside', says Jesus in Mark 17.21, 'out of a man's heart, come evil thoughts, acts of fornication, of theft, murder, adultery, ruthless greed and malice.' Promiscuity and profiteering – the Bible continually brackets these two types of excess. 'Put to death those parts of you which belong to the earth – fornication, indecency, lust, foul cravings and the ruthless greed which is nothing less than idolatry' (Col. 3.5).

The opposite of this lust for possession and domination is the readiness to fit one's own needs to the needs of others and to submit self-assertion to the claims of an equipoise society. The word is moderation (*epieikēs*), and there is a small but important point of grammar to be noted here. In Greek there are two verbs with the root *eik-*, one meaning to yield and the other (of which several parts were obsolete) meaning to be alike. It is from this second root that we get the word *ikon*, a likeness, and it is from that root also that this word, *epieikēs*, is derived. So moderation is not, as some of the translations seem to suppose, a yielding meekness; it means, rather, a matching, a toning in with the whole, an awareness of how one's own small piece fits into the jigsaw picture.

This virtue of *epieikēs*, or fitting oneself into the total frame of reference, is the 'moderation' of the good Christian which should be evident to all men (Philippians 4.4). In that verse the Revised Version translates the word as 'forbearance', Phillips suggests 'gentleness', and the New English Bible has 'magnanimity'. It is a very significant concept, linked, I believe, with the doctrine of creation. In that supremely important passage, Colossians, 1.16–17, the totality of things (*ta panta*) is said to have been created and to be put together by the Beloved Son. The second of those two words is also used in II Peter 3.5–6 which, referring again to the creation, speaks of the earth as being put together or held together 'out of water and amidst water'. That is meant to conjure up the image of God gathering together the waters into their allotted place and setting the bounds of the dry land (Genesis 1.9–10). This setting of boundaries and allocation of parts in relation to the whole is emphasized in the vivid poetry of Psalm 104:

> At thy rebuke they ran, at the sound of thy thunder they rushed away, flowing over the hills, pouring down into the valleys to the place appointed for them. Thou didst fix a boundary which they might not pass; they shall not return to cover the earth.

That last phrase is a reminder of the time of judgment when the waters *did* return and cover the earth in Noah's flood, to which the passage in II Peter also refers. The earth, held together in the midst of the water yet separate from the water, was overwhelmed by the water when once the divine boundaries, fitting the parts into the whole, were overrun.

That sense of the totality of creation and the fitness of each part in proper proportion to the rest, is the reverse of the narrow-visioned sin of *pleonexia* which, disregarding the whole, grasps at excess and throws everything out of balance. True to this doctrine of creation, which modern ecology has strikingly endorsed, the disciple of Christ proclaims the kingdom of right relationships and calls on all men to make their far-reaching financial decisions with a sense of accountability for the whole system under God. Our concept of 'goods' must always include and yet distinguish between the primary goods (water, minerals, forests, energy, etc.), which may be either renewable or non-renewable, and secondary goods, which we produce from the primary either in the form of manufactures or of services. Each of these categories is essentially different from each of the others, yet our system of accounting is bound to lose touch with reality if it disregards any one of the four.

If, to take a merely symbolic example, a company destroys many square miles of valuable forest and makes 10,000 coffins, it *should* seem patently absurd to credit the total transaction to the gross national product! Or, to take another example which is no flight of fancy, a well-known company produces 9 million articles a year, knowing that the demand for and actual use of these articles cannot exceed 5 million. The further 4 million are necessary for 'growth', though they meet no need. They have to be pushed (with a commission on sales) as courtesy Christmas presents which other firms may buy to distribute to their business associates. But any system of accounting which can describe as 'growth' 4 million articles thrown new-made into waste-paper baskets must be deliberately blinding itself to the reality of the whole. Sir John Lawrence was pleading for a more truly inclusive reckoning of profit and loss when he wrote to the editor of *The Times* in January 1973:

What I want to do is question whether there is not a need to reconsider the fundamental ground rules of economic performance if we are really to preserve the national *human* resource . . . All of our present measures are ways of assessing the inflow and outflow of cash or, broadly, the return on the capital resource. But businesses use other resources and we seem not to be seriously concerned as to whether we use these well . . . The problem, as I see it, is to find some way of . . . recognizing that a company that develops the abilities of its employees for purposeful ends is a more valuable company than one that does not. . . . Ideas are beginning to develop of human asset or human resource for counting. The need is for companies to experiment with the con-

47

cept, to build on what has begun, to find out the difficulties of making some estimation of changes in the value of human resources.

I Timothy 3.3 contrasts this virtue of fitting in with the twin excesses of brawling and money-grubbing. II Corinthians 7.2 describes the blamelessness of the author's ministry in three negatives: we have injured no one, we have spoiled no one, we have not taken more than our fair share. There again is that root idea of excess: taking more, spending more than is justified in a delicately balanced system, failing to fit in because of failure to be aware. The New Testament dream reflects, of course, the character of Christ himself; but essentially, it is a projection of the Old Testament dream in which self-assertion is swallowed up in awareness of the whole community and the whole system and its reciprocity, and that in turn stems from the even more intense awareness of the God who creates the system and the community through the gift of his covenant, his own reciprocity with man.

It is against that background that we must learn to discern the extreme danger of any simple definitions of function or aim which betray the blinkered vision or the one-track obsessive motivation. The man who breathes the spirit of the covenant and tries to observe the moderation of fitting each part into the living whole is going to find himself compelled to ask simple but rather disturbing questions about almost all our assumptions and axioms. Take, for example, the phrase I have already raged at in an earlier chapter: that it is the primary function of industry to create wealth. Does man, industrial or otherwise, create? Creation means making something out of nothing, which is why we have usually been taught that only God can create. I am not splitting theological hairs. The use of that word with regard to industry is a blinker, limiting vision so we miss an important part of the whole. The products of industry are never made out of nothing. Say, rather, that the primary function of industry is to convert certain materials into wealth, and immediately you have taken off one of the blinkers and allowed the forests, the minerals, the soil, the animals, or whatever other part of the whole you are drawing on, to come into your view and into your answerability. For these are one of the resources you are investing in the business of converting something into something else. And there you have lifted another verbal blinker. When we speak of investing in a company we usually mean only the money put in by the shareholders. But that is only one of three kinds of investment that are put into every enterprise; the other two are the raw materials, which I have just mentioned, and people. The workers in a factory or business are *human* assets. At that point at least every worker is a shareholder; he is putting something far more irreplaceable than money into the business. And by putting himself into it he earns the right to ask what return he gets for his investment. Wages and security is part of the answer; but a good business is expected to *develop* its assets, and as this blinker is taken off, more and more firms are coming to see how important, and in the truest sense profitable, is this obligation to develop their human assets. And so one goes on, relating such ideas as profitability or wealth to this vision of the whole system under God, and finding that their meanings are immediately expanded. That is what I mean by balance. That is what I have in mind when I speak of equipoise as a better word than either equality or equity. I think there is something of this broad vision in St Paul's enthusiasm for the collection from the Gentile congregations and its offering by representatives of those churches to the motherland in Jerusalem:

> There is no question of relieving others at the cost of hardship to yourselves; it is a question of equality. At the moment your surplus meets their need, but one day your need may be met from their surplus. The aim is equality; as Scripture has it, 'The man who got much had no more than enough, and the man who got little did not go short' (II Corinthians 8.15).

That quotation at the end refers of course to a story that was an important object lesson in the theology of enough, the story of the mystical manna which God gave to his people even before he had given them the law. 'What is that?' they asked. And the answer was crucial: 'That is the bread which the Lord has given you to eat.' God's gift, and man's happy dependence upon it, is the ground of the theology of enough. It is graciousness born of grace. 'Each of you is to gather as much as he can eat.' There an important note is struck: the covenant does not call for asceticism. Nor do I believe that we, in our day, should seek a deliberate return to poverty. It is not poverty but balance we are after, and balance, I believe, may well mean for us in the affluent countries a reduction in our standard of living. But it would be an absurd exaggeration to say that for three-quarters of our population in Britain a reduction of standard would come anywhere near poverty. So in this object lesson of the early Hebrews the story of the mysterious manna goes on: 'Those who had gathered more had not too much, and those who had gathered less had not too little.' And those who tried hoarding it found that it bred maggots and stank. It is that stink which rises today from all over our despoiled environment.

### The non-violent dominion

The ideal that is expressed mystically in this symbol of the manna in the wilderness was worked out practically in the laws that were to govern the settled life of the kingdom, particularly in the book of Deuteronomy.

There is the law of gleaning. The Hebrew farmer is not to be mean or over-careful. He must not reap to the very edges of his fields (remember those hedgerows!), nor cut the loose stalks that fall free of the swathe, nor go back for the odd sheaf which has been left behind on the field. When beating his olives he must not go over the boughs a second time; neither may he completely strip his vineyard nor gather the fallen fruit. 'What is left shall be for the alien, the orphan and the widow. I am the Lord your God.' That is to say: remember what kind of God I am; remember the world of human and ecological relationships in which you enjoy the covenant with me. Enough is enough, and the less fortunate will be glad of what is left. The reason for this moderation is the memory of their own dependency. They are not self-made men: they owe everything to God. 'Remember that you were slaves in Egypt; *that* is why I command you to do this' (Leviticus 19.9–10; Deuteronomy 25.19–22).

What a contrast to the terms in which the manufacturers of a combine-harvester advertise their product today! We have made a virtue of scraping the barrel and squeezing the last drop, so a law against taking the mother bird as well as its young, or against preventing an ox from taking its mouthful as it treads the corn, strikes us as merely quaint (Deuteronomy 22.6; 25.4).

But the biblical theology of enough cannot be expressed in negatives. It is a very positive ideal, enshrined in the Pentateuch, just as the 'Kingdom' is enshrined in the parables of Jesus. Just as many Jews may have failed to keep the different precepts as Christians have failed to turn the other cheek and invite unknown handicapped people to their parties. But the ideal was there, as distinctive and attractive as a half-forgotten dream or a fragrance or a taste – and how often the metaphor of taste is used to describe the way of the law. We are dealing with a way of life which God's minority is called to take as its standard in the midst of the world for the sake of God's majority. That is the significance for us of this old Hebrew life-style. We cannot evade its implications for ourselves simply by dismissing it as an agrarian culture of a past age which must be totally inapplicable in our case. Unless, as we have a perfect right to do, we dissociate ourselves entirely from the religion which takes the Bible as its scriptures, we are bound to take seriously the unifying thread which runs through all those scriptures and binds them together. And that thread is the idea that when God set about redeeming the whole of his creation he chose those Hebrew people, liberated them from slavery and gave them a pattern to live by in order that through them all the nations of the world might be blessed. Christians say that this promise was fulfilled in Jesus Christ. But when Jesus came preaching the kingdom he was opening up to the entire world that Kingdom of right relationships which long ago God had invited that one special nation to enter and enjoy. If we take the Bible seriously at all, then we must take seriously the idea that what was first offered to Israel was meant to be a model of the salvation that was to be experienced in the end by all. And we would say the same of the Christian church in the world today. Of course the details will be entirely different because the cultures are different; only the cranks would deny that. But the style of relationship, the order of priorities, the criteria and the frame of reference, these are valid still and their demand on us has to be faced. And if our response is to take these things as the standard of our life-style, then we shall see in this old law of gleaning a sign of an essentially courteous and generous relationship between man and nature, between man and his fellow men and, essentially, between man and God.

Then there is the law of limited cropping. The soil of the holy land is not to be over-exploited, the vines are quite enough for the vineyard to nourish: there must be no planting between the lines (Deuteronomy 22.9). Every seventh year the fields must lie fallow, and vineyards and olive gardens be left unpruned; the crop that grows from the last year's fallen grain and the grapes on the unpruned vines are to provide food for the poor who have not been able to lay up for this year of the land's release (Exodus 23.10–11; Leviticus 25.1–7).

This is an aspect of the sabbath which Protestant theology has almost entirely missed. The familiar words of the sabbath commandment come from Exodus 20. In Exodus 23 there is a somewhat different version with rather more stress on the altruistic motive, which is generally believed to have come from an earlier code of regulations:

> For six days you may do your work, but on the seventh day you shall abstain from work, so that your ox and your ass may rest, and your home-born slave and the alien may refresh themselves.

But notice how this weekly cycle is the echo of a seven year cycle which has been ordered in the preceding verse in an exactly similar pattern of words.

> For six years you may sow your land and gather its produce; but in the seventh year you shall let it lie fallow and leave it alone. It shall

provide food for the poor of your people, and what they leave, the wild animals may eat. You shall do likewise with your vineyard and your olive-grove.

It seems to me highly probable that the form that is finally given to the Hebrew folk-stories about the first man reflects the dream that for so many centuries had dominated the ideals and aspirations of the people and had been embodied in their social laws. Adam, made in the likeness of the creator, male and female in his fullness, is set as God's vicegerent in the world. That, according to this account, is the point at which he bears the image of God. 'Then God said, "Let us make man in our image and likeness to rule the fish in the sea, the birds of heaven, the cattle, all wild animals on earth, and all reptiles that crawl upon the earth." So God created man in his own image.' But the quality of his dominion over nature is intended to reflect the quality of God's dominion – loving, cherishing and essentially self-giving. That is how it will be so long as, in all his exercise of power, he is answerable to God, seeing that he is himself a creature. 'Thou hast made him little lower than God, crowning him with glory and honour.' Only in his unbroken awareness of God is man's technological mastery safe. Only in his acceptance of creature-hood can his dominion be prevented from becoming raw domination. For being answerable to God, he remains answerable for his fellow creatures and for the soil of his earth. 'The Lord God took the man and put him in the garden to till it and care for it.' But enough is enough, and answerability means the acceptance of limits. 'You may eat from every tree in the garden but not from the tree of the knowledge of good and evil.' Adam can be trusted with so vast a sovereignty so long as he knows how to take no for an answer. The earth and all its resources are for you to exploit and develop *but* there is a time for the earth to regather its strength and there are others than yourself to be considered. The days and the weeks are yours to make and build and trade *but* there is a time to stand back and take stock in relation to the needs of the whole, and especially those on whose energies you rely. Yes, all the trees in the garden are yours *but* – enough is enough.

Isn't that the cosmic equivalent of the historical injunction to that small particular people, 'Remember that you have been slaves in Egypt and the Lord your God redeemed you from there, that is why I command you to do this'? The denial of the absolute always leads to alienation from the contingent.

The law of the first-fruits is another check on excess. We take it for granted that the first of the early potatoes will be expensive. Our grandparents built the *Cutty Sark* and its beautiful rival sailing ships to compete for the first lading of tea to reach the London market each year. But in the kingdom of God a potato is a potato is a potato, and making a profit out of rarity is forbidden in the law of the ancient Hebrews, as in many other cultures which we, from our commercial superiority, call 'primitive'. So the first reaping of new corn, the first bottling of wine and oil, the first-born lambs or calves, and even the firstborn sons, must be set aside for God. In doing this the Hebrew farmer again commemorates his humble dependence upon his Redeemer: 'My father was a homeless Aramean who went down to Egypt with a small company . . . so the Lord brought us out of Egypt with a strong hand and outstretched arm . . . and now I have brought the first-fruits of the soil which thou, O Lord, hast given me' (Exodus 22.29; 23.16; Deuteronomy 26.1–11).

This prohibition on snatching the chance of a high price because of the scarcity of the first-fruits is in flat contradiction to the accepted principle of supply and demand. Tawney's great book, *Religion and the Rise of Capitalism*, showed that the medieval church denied the validity of the law of supply and demand in favour of that other principle we have already noted both in the Old and New Testaments, the principle of an equipoise society and the condemnation of any unfair advantage which would immediately upset the delicate balance of interdependence and responsibility. The stern pressure of circumstances are compelling us at last to recognize how essential is this balance in what we call an eco-system. But that is only a reflection of the balance which is equally essential for the true functioning of the even vaster system in which God, man and the rest of nature, the past the present and the future, are held together, the kingdom of right relationships.

St Thomas Aquinas taught that 'A contract is fair when both parties gain from it equally'. What a difference that would make to our negotiations with Sri Lanka over the price of tea or between management and labour in industrial disputes. St Raymond in the thirteenth century included in the sins of 'unfair advantage' not only the taking of interest for a loan, but the raising of prices by a monopolist, the beating down of prices by a keen bargainer, the rack-renting of land by a landlord, the sub-letting of land by a tenant at a rent higher than he himself paid, the cutting of wages or the paying of wages in truck, the refusal of discount to a tardy debtor, the insistence on unreasonably good security on a loan, the excessive profits of a middle man. It is a long time since any political party proposed such a list of bills as that in the Speech from the Throne! I am not suggesting that the economics of the thirteenth century provide any sort of blueprint for us in our own day. But we are neither so confident nor so agreed about our own economic theory that we cannot at least take note of the tough, agile intelligence with which those old boys wrestled to relate the facts of their world to the frame of reference which they believed the Bible offered them. Bishop Barry, that grand old witness to the eternal relevance of the scriptures, wrote in *The Times* in March 1973:

> We need a new Christian philosophy of money. How far are there any moral considerations in the distribution of the rewards of industry? The demand for 'fairness' in prices and incomes policy suggests some conviction that there are, or should be, and that market price should not be the sole criterion. But what is 'fair'? What does a man deserve? The mediaeval church made the attempt, in a simpler agrarian community, to lay down a just price and a just wage. But it has never been properly rethought. The church can offer no useful moral guidance if it allows the forms of the debate to be distorted by purely technical arguments.

There is another important aspect of that old law of the Hebrews that the rare, pricey first-fruits were not to be exploited on the market but set aside for God. It reminds us that the background of the whole of life under the old covenant was the sacrificial system. All must be offered continually to God, for all belongs to God, and man prospers only through God's goodness and mercy. This is what it meant to live by grace under that old dispensation. The system was intended to preclude arrogance and greed. In this respect there was no conflict between the priests and the prophets.

The attitude engendered by Israel's covenant with God found, as we have seen, a universal expression in the creation story as Israel learned to tell it. Man is seen as God's viceroy in the world. His mandate to control and civilize is dependent on his answerability as a creature towards his Creator. When man rejects his responsible sonship he turns into the anxiously assertive spoilt child who must at all costs have his own way. His God-given essentially non-violent dominion over nature becomes raving domination. Technology is safe only in a context of worship, and science should walk hand in hand with sacrifice.

### *What news on the Rialto?*

I think that what I have just said is also the background to a fourth group of laws in the Old Testament that are relevant to the biblical view we are trying to assess, the prohibition against charging interest on loans. Some of the passages which speak of this law make no reference to the kind of persons to whom loans are made, others seem to assume that it will always be someone who is in a spot and definitely in need of help; the assumption seems to be that debtors will be among the poor and vulnerable. Then again, in some passages a distinction is made and the law of interest-free loans is seen to apply only to fellow-Israelites, that is to say to those who stand in the same covenant. Foreign creditors are excluded from the interest-free clause. Exodus 20.25 says, 'If you advance money to any poor man among my people you shall not act like a money lender, you must not exact interest in advance from him.' Deuteronomy 23.20 distinguishes between oans to fellow-countrymen and loans to foreigners, presumably because of the greater need for some security or compensation, though it may be simply because this whole system of give-and-take in the network of mutual caring and responsibility was felt to extend only to those who were under the covenant and therefore separated as a model. In that case, if the covenant is opened up to the whole world, then the principle of the interest-free loan becomes universally applicable. At the time of the exile the prophet Ezekiel, that great dreamer of the ideal society, presents his portrait of 'the man who is righteous and does what is just and right'. This portrayal seems no more to limit the prohibition on interest to fellow-countrymen than it does with any of the other phrases.

> He oppresses no man, he returns the debtor's pledge, he never robs. He gives bread to the hungry and clothes to those who have none. He never lends either at discount or at interest. He shuns injustice and deals fairly between man and man (Ezekiel 18.16–17).

The taking of a pledge as security for the repayment of a loan is permitted, though it must be stated that the words in which this is referred to almost invariably seem to assume a short-term loan for which the pledge is more like some household possession offered in pawn. In this matter there are frequent injunctions against harshness in the taking of a pledge. Deuteronomy 24.10–11 forbids intrusion into a house, and verse 6 in the same chapter excludes the taking of anything that is vital for the other man's daily living. It is also worth noting that the jailing of a debtor, referred to in the parables of Jesus, was unknown in Jewish law and has a Hellenistic and Roman rather than a Semitic background.

For reasons I have already given, I do not believe that a Christian today can simply dismiss this biblical prohibition as of no consequence to modern society. However the details may change, scripture is clear that something is inherently liable to go wrong in the charging of interest on loans. Even if we decide in good conscience that interest is permissible, we should surely set our face against any high rates of interest, especially with regard to mortgages and hire purchase.

It is interesting to see how seriously the church took these prohibitions on interest, and the significance of this fact cannot be ignored. At the Council of Arles in 314 and again at the famous Council of Nicea in 325 all clerics were forbidden to take interest on loans, and the later Councils at Carthage in 348 and at Aix in 789 objected even to laymen charging interest. The Third Lateran Council in 1179 and the Second Council of Lyons in 1274 formally condemned all interest on loans. It was in order to get around this prohibition that Western monarchs ironically invited Jews into their countries to be the money-lenders, giving them virtually no opportunities to be anything else! Medieval theology and philosophy related this prohibition not only to the regulations in the Old Testament but also to Aristotle's doctrine that by nature money is 'barren', that is to say that it is *only* a medium of exchange made by man for his convenience. The resources of the world – its raw materials and living things – are all creatures of God with the capacity of fruitfulness both in nature and in the use that man makes of them. But it is against nature to force money itself to beget money. Even after the Reformation Luther and Zwingli and the Anglican divines throughout the sixteenth century condemned the charging of interest on loans, though in 1571 the *civil* law in England provided for moderate charges of interest to be made. Even as late as 1634 the Irish church included in its canons the proviso that the person who charged interest on his loans, like the adulterer, should be subjected to ecclesiastical discipline.

But at this point I would say that I believe the church made the fatal mistake of trying to argue casuistically in order to keep particular regulations and institutions in force in a changed world instead of arguing in visual images with reference back to the basic scheme of relationships which underlay those older regulations. They ask, for example, does a ban on extortionate money-lending extend to the investment of capital in company shares? The issue was not really confused until investment in an enterprise ceased to be a personal participation with a personal stake and became a money transaction several removes from the business in which one had a stake. It is one thing to go shares with a few enterprising neighbours to buy a cow or a boat, risk losing your capital and take your slice of the earnings. It is a very different thing to instruct your broker to buy shares in Blue Star Line. The real question is, can we keep the older image sufficiently vivid in our minds to feel that our investments are not monies loaned on interest but partnership both in risk and profit? Perhaps there is a clue here worth following up at this moment when many economists are calling for a new international monetary system. We are adrift without some such image or model from which we can argue. And that was the trouble with the church as it faced all the new challenges of the rise of capitalism. Tawney has shown us how it was that a short-sighted commercial expediency finally won the day.

> Shocked, confused, thrown on to a helpless, if courageous and eloquent, defensive . . . mediaeval social theory . . . found itself swept off its feet . . . by the swift rise of a commercial civilization, in which all traditional landmarks seemed one by one to be submerged.[3]

One reason for that failure, I believe, was that the church had become so institutionalized in its thinking that it tried to use casuistry to show how old regulations could themselves be twisted sufficiently to become applicable to the new circumstances. What is needed at a moment of immense rapid change is not legal detail but a renewed visual image of the whole framework which had originally given the meanings to those legal details. That is why I am calling for a return to some model, some picture which takes the whole range of man's existence into account. And I still believe that the kingdom of right relationships, the society of the *shalom* of God, which was offered to mankind in the covenant he made with the Hebrew people, and later lived out in personal dimensions and made available to the whole world in Christ, is valid for the deep perplexities of our own day.

In the kingdom of right relationships, as the Hebrews were inspired to see it and prepared to embody it in their laws, there is much more that bears out this theology of enough, and almost always the reason given for these merciful limitations on man's aggressive ruthlessness is the same as before: 'Remember that you were slaves in Egypt and the Lord your God redeemed you from there.' Enough is enough, and there are limits to what you may expect or demand; limits set by consideration for the other and by a recognition of your own place in the whole scheme of things.

## Eucharistic living

But there is another aspect of the theology of enough which comes as a surprise when we meet it in the Old Testament and which predominates in the New. It appears most clearly in the law of tithing. This, of course, is another device to set limits to selfish excess. In addition to the first-fruits, a full tenth of a farmer's annual produce has to be dedicated to God for the support of what we would call the parochial ministry and also for the less fortunate members of society (Numbers 18.21–29; Deuteronomy 26.12–15). The observance of the tithe might easily produce a tight-lipped self-righteousness such as Jesus attributed to the praying Pharisee in his parable. But to think of the tithe as an act of self-denial was to miss the whole point of it. It was intended to be a most almighty beano, a party to celebrate the Lord's generosity.

> Year by year you shall set aside a tithe of all the produce of your seed, of everything that grows on the land. You shall eat it in the presence of the Lord your God . . . When the journey (*to Jerusalem*) is too great for you to be able to carry your tithe, then you may exchange it for silver. You shall tie up the silver and take it with you to the place which the Lord your God will choose. There you shall spend it as you will, on cattle or sheep, wine or strong drink, or whatever you desire; you shall consume it there with rejoicing, both you and your family in the presence of the Lord your God. You must not neglect the Levites who live in your settlements (Deuteronomy 14.22–27).

A spending-spree, whisky and all, to make our commercial Christmas look like a Lenten fast! That was their way of saying thank you to God. Such spontaneous, lavish celebration is the absolute opposite of the greedy spirit of grasping, hoarding, exploiting and turning everything back into greater profits. And this generosity to oneself goes hand in hand with generosity to those who are less fortunate or less secure.

> At the end of every third year you shall bring out all the tithe of your produce for that year, and leave it in your settlements so that the Levites, who have no holding or patrimony among you, and the aliens, orphans, and widows in your settlements, may come and eat their fill. If you do this, the Lord your God will bless you in everything to which you set your hand (Deuteronomy 14.28–29).

In those centuries when the peoples of Europe tried to model their public life on the insights of the Bible, there were a great many holidays, all of them were religious, and all were feast-days. Every great house, and even the homes of the moderately well-to-do, extended the hospitality of the feast to embrace, as of right, the poor and the ne'er-do-wells, the immigrants and the homeless.

The prodigal son remembered his father's home as the place where even the lowest paid servant had 'enough and to spare', and this is the emphasis which the New Testament gives to the theology of enough. Excess is not simply prohibited; it is replaced by a lavish generosity of both give and take.

> Give, and gifts will be given to you. Good measure, pressed down, shaken together, and running over, will be poured into your lap; for whatever measure you deal out to others will be dealt to you in return (Luke 6.38).

The great breakthrough of the New Testament is that the generosities of the old covenant are extended to all men. They are no longer an expression of family or tribal or religious solidarity; so they are no longer restricted to a limited circle only. They are for all men in all circumstances and in every place. Such is the unbounded liberality and fellowship of what might be called 'the eucharistic life', the life that is built on gratitude, or rather on an intense awareness of him who is to be thanked.

But the life of Jesus and his disciples was not only eucharistic but also defiant. He knew it was not enough to say these things; the world was waiting for concrete examples and realizations. So in our day it is not enough to point out the contrast between our idolatry of growth and the Bible's theology of enough; we have to opt out of the drift and help one another to live in cheerful protest against it. We have to discover what fun it can be to defy the blandishments and undermine the assumptions of the excessive consumer society.

Someone or other will accuse us of 'dropping out' at the expense of society. When that happens, we might try reading to our accuser this extract from a circular sent by post in the autumn of 1974 advertising an investment advice service.

These are the sorts of subjects we will be dealing with:
    How to guard against hyper-inflation
    The fastest-growing agricultural land syndicates
    Investor's guide to Chinese ceramics
    Two investment ideas to beat estate duty
    Should you join a bloodstock syndicate?
    How to play the stockmarket in New York and Toronto
    Buying jewellery with an eye to eventual profit
    What questions to ask when buying property abroad
    Investing in carriage clocks
    How to beat the resale problems in fine art
    Where to buy vineyards in Italy and France
    Which are the leading tax-haven banks?
    Why to buy an annuity denominated in foreign currency

Who are the drop-outs now?

# 4

## *The Cheerful Revolution*

It'll be no use their putting their heads down and saying, 'Come up again, dear!' I shall only look up and say, 'Who am I then? Tell me that first, and then, if I like being that person, I'll come up: if not, I'll stay down here till I'm somebody else.'

*Alice's Adventures in Wonderland*

### *The pressures confronting us*

Things have to change. We cannot go on as we are. Whether we look at our situation in the light of the Bible's vision and values; or in terms of the simple calculation that, in a world of limited resources, in order that others may have more, we must be content with comparatively less; or in the recognition that a frenetic consumer society breeds ever more violent techniques and ever deeper stress in its citizens; we know that we have to call a halt to this kind of so-called 'development'.

At this point, facing the inevitable outcry of 'nonsense!' or worse, it is easy to fall into despair and to say that it is too much to expect the industrialized and growth-oriented countries to accept a deceleration in their own material output while, at the same time, substantially helping the poorer nations in their efforts to advance their economies more rapidly; and certainly far too optimistic to expect any political party to go to the country with a manifesto offering a standard of living lower in cash terms though higher in human satisfaction. Perhaps we ought to find a wry sense of encouragement from the very speed and sharpness of the reaction to our suggestions. I cannot be sure whether the two were connected, but the fact is that very soon after I published a *News-Letter* with the same title as this book which led to the organization of a student conference in the USA under the same title, a large advertisement was placed in some of our national dailies in the name of a particular firm, showing a business executive wearing an outsize lapel button bearing the motto: Enough is *not* Enough! If such quick response indicates that we have hit a sore spot, then we must hit it again and again. For it is in the area of public opinion that this battle has to be fought. Nothing will achieve the change of policies which our very salvation demands but a profound re-orientation of public opinion. Jeremy Bugler comes to this conclusion at the end of his book *Polluting Britain*:

> What the offensive against pollution needs in Britain is not only new laws, not only new agencies, not only new taxes and new technologies, but new attitudes.

Early in 1972 Reg Prentice, a former Minister of Overseas Development, made the same point about the way in which Britain's concern for the under-developed nations might be improved:

> The rich countries are so preoccupied with sorting out their relations with each other that they do not have much time left for the remaining two-thirds of the human family. There is only one way to counteract this: slow, hard grind of public education and political pressure within the rich countries.

It is significant also that the final paragraph of the United Nations General Assembly's resolution inaugurating the Second Development Decade from 1 January 1971 was entitled *Mobilization of Public Opinion*.

There lies the Christian's greatest opportunity and challenge. It is not enough to talk. Our Western societies are sick of moralizing about world poverty. We need a thoughtful, convinced minority that will *live* in such a way as to challenge the cherished beliefs of the consumer society and defy its compulsions. In order to live differently we first need a *rationale*, and for this I have already looked back to the Bible and found, not a blueprint nor a precise code of regulations, but a habit of dealing with each particular objective with eyes wide open to the total context of relationships and responsibilities. And then, having found this biblical *rationale*, it is not enough merely to say 'That was an interesting Bible study,' and promptly flutter on to some other topic. We need to study the Bible text, preferably in groups, until we have made its basic frame of reference our own and can instinctively apply it to our contemporary situations. We should try to become as naturally at home in this God-centred and world-embracing way of looking at things as a good Marxist is in his quite different ideology. Only so can we guard the freedom of our minds against the insidious pressures that are being brought to bear upon them from all sides.

Let us not underestimate the power of those pressures to force us willy-nilly to accept unthinkingly all the assumptions of the industrialized consumer society. We don't have to believe all Vance Packard's grisly warnings about an infallible science of advertising laying siege to our subconscious. In his *Techniques of Persuasion*,[2] J. A. C. Brown shows that the ordinary person has proved to be more resilient against such methods of persuasion than was at first thought likely. And Sinclair Baker tells a delightful story about a corn products company which tried to sell its confectionery with this television jingle:

I love Bosco,
It's rich and choc'lat-y.
Momma puts it in my milk
Because it's good for me.

After a while reports started coming in from all over the nation that were rather disturbing to the advertiser. A favourite song heard in school playgrounds and wherever the kids gathered was:

I hate Bosco,
It's full of TNT.

Momma puts it in my milk
To try to poison me.

Yet the significant fact is that the producers, who are not accustomed to throwing good money after bad, continue to spend more and more astronomical figures on advertising. They must believe that it accomplishes something. And of course they are right. Advertising helps enormously to create the consumer mood. It keeps things, and the value of getting things, continually before the public's eye. It doesn't matter much which version of the jingle the children are singing in their playgrounds so long as they are singing about confectionery that is available in the sweetshop down the road and not about Miss Muffett's purely mythical curds and whey. Even if a TV advertisement does not persuade a viewer to buy the particular brand that it recommends, it will increase the sales of the product as a whole – breakfast cereals or beer or shampoo in general. And that is all the promoters of consumption are really after. The apparent cut-throat competition between one brand and another is often an entirely phoney war. Sinclair Baker instances an announcement of unusual courtesy which a particular shoe manufacturer inserted in the press.

> The Weyenberg Shoe Company wishes the Portage Shoe Company lots of luck . . . without going into a whole treatise on the economics of competition, the Portage people have really kept us on our toes. We have had to come to grips with the fact that they make a fine shoe, and that makes us make ours a little finer.[3]

What the public were not told was that both brands were owned by the same corporation. The impression of hard-hitting competition convinced a knowing public that it must be getting its shoes at cut-price rates.

John Poulton, in *People Under Pressure*, says:

> Today we are likely to suffer all seven assaults upon our consciousness at once, by TV commercial, by posters, by coupon through the letter-box, by national newspaper advertisements, by lead-line display in several local shops, by local newspaper ads with cut-out coupon for cash-off enticements to quicker sales, and by actually seeing the pro-

duct on a neighbour's kitchen table. Somewhere along the line we have lost the will to ask 'why?' any more. Why must my sights be raised constantly beyond what would be sufficient for me and mine? Why must I continue to be edged along into expecting more and more of life quantifiably measured in goods and services?[4]

Why indeed? But the blackmail grows more insistent. It appeals to our fear of becoming odd in other people's eyes, losing respect, dropping behind. The free-handout magazines, aimed at recently recruited typists or girls just leaving school, which are thrust into the hands of commuters as they leave the main London stations, are filled with this level of approach. 'The price is £2·40, but you won't mind if you fancy a touch of class!' Or 'Accessories can make or mar any outfit and if you spend quite a bit of money on them they never let you down.' And in an earlier chapter I pointed out how much of the advertising of the car industry appeals to the pathetic longing of individuals to steal a march on their fellows and assert a recognizable identity so as not to be submerged in the faceless competitive tide. 'The rat race is for rats,' cries Jimmy Reid in passionate anger. 'We are not rats. We are human beings!'

The message which is proclaimed to the little typists through the free-handout magazines is dinned into all of us in one way or another. Our power of resistance will depend to a considerable extent upon our ability to stop and analyse what the message is actually saying. Peter Challen of the South London Industrial Mission has pointed out to me how our growing global consciousness is reflected in an increasingly frequent use of the globe itself as a symbol or as a visual pun in advertising. A recent colour supplement, for example, showed, floating in deep purple space like a sunlit planet, a globe constructed entirely of timber packing cases and stamped with the trade name 'British Airways Cargo'. Underneath is the arrogant message: 'Now the world is ours.' The message that the world consists of goods for the getting comes across loud and clear. The same acquisitive note is struck even more crudely in a photo-print advertisement for ECGD showing a globe resting like a round fruit on a table top beside a lemon squeezer. Yet another, advertising BC wood products, shows a circle divided in two, the lower half containing part of the map of the northern hemisphere, the upper half marked with uneven concentric rings like the end of a newly-sawn log – an entertaining fancy for an international timber company, until one remembers what is the real price of our plundering of the world's forests. Each of those three advertisements, in fact, is skilfully propagating the profoundly false attitudes by which the prophets of growth want us all to live. They are false, as I tried to show in the last chapter, because they insist on fitting global aspirations into a pathetically blinkered and self-interested frame of reference. Peter Challen calls all such enterprises 'an international movement with a localized vocation'.

### Joyful resistance movement

Those are the interests and that the philosophy against which we have to organize our light-hearted revolution. I say 'light-hearted' with deliberation because I am sure that once we begin to take ourselves too seriously we offer our opponent too many hand-holds. Theodore Roszak wrote:

> Nothing counts more heavily against the technocracy than a successful desertion, for there is no underestimating the influence of an authentically happy disaffiliate in a society of affluent self-contempt. Every drop-out who drops into a freer, more joyous, more self-determining style of life – a style of life that *works* – breaks the paralysing official consensus.[5]

The same feeling that only defiance can save us now was expressed by a young Japanese poet, Kaneko Mitsuharu in the 1950s:

> When I'm asked for what I was born,
> Without scruple, I'll reply: 'To oppose.'
> When I'm in the east
> I want to go to the west.
>
> I fasten my coat at the left, my shoes right and left.
> My hakama I wear back to front and I ride a horse facing its buttocks.

What everyone else hates I like
And my greatest hate of all is people feeling the same.

This I believe: to oppose
Is the only thing in life.
To oppose is to live.
To oppose is to get a grip on the very self.[6]

Light-hearted we must be if we want to elude the manipulators and survive; but let us never forget the ruthlessness of those principalities and powers against which we fight. If the inevitable changes are to come about in our society voluntarily and without ghastly catastrophe, nothing will achieve them but a profound change of public opinion. Our Western malaise is one of attitudes, values and expectations rather than one of methods and systems. Yet, inasmuch as the systems often impose the attitudes, we have to defy them also; and this calls for a counter-culture of families and groups that cannot be conned or manipulated because they simply do not accept the accepted values or pursue the ambitions that are expected of them. We must try to live by the divine contrariness of Jesus. We need a rapidly increasing minority that is entirely counter-suggestible, a minority that calls the bluff of the trend-setters, is a dead loss to the advertising agencies and poor material for the careers advisers. We must not wait for all Christians to be persuaded of the need for this, neither should we waste our time designing a single rule of life for those who are so persuaded. If we are trying to create a climate of social non-conformity we must avoid moralizing like the plague. Our need is for men and women who are free with the freedom of Christ, free to ask the awkward questions that have occurred to no one else, and free to come up with startling answers that no one else has dared to give.

The difficulty of what I want to say now is that it could so easily fall into a nagging series of 'oughts' and 'ought nots', and that is the very opposite of the spirit I want to engender. All I shall try to do is to hold out a number of lines that different people may be moved to take up and follow. One will appeal to some and another to others, but they have a certain common style, and cumulatively they could add up to a way of life – a way of life rather than of death.

I suggest as a start the acceptance of a motto appropriate to a battered but glorious coat of arms: *The price tag is too high.* Often we shall have to apply these words quite literally. As a family we can't afford a colour TV or a continental holiday, and the car will have to do another two years at least. We haven't needed them, scarcely wanted them, up to now, and no amount of sales-talk is going to persuade us that we need them now. If last year's luxuries become this year's necessities, our income will need to go up a lot quicker; but why on earth should it? Why be conned into joining the inflationary rat-race? We don't have to keep up with the Joneses. Let them draw ahead until they are out of sight; for us the price tag is too high. If a few million citizens could learn to have fun with that simple slogan we would be moving a lot nearer to a stabilized cost-of-living index, and the manufacturers would be compelled to turn their ingenuity to more productive and humanly useful goods.

But there are other senses in which we shall often have to apply our motto, The price tag is too high. If the exercise of my right to drive my car by myself into the inner city contributes to the inefficiency and high cost of public transport and worsens the housing shortage by devouring more precious land in new road space, then the price tag on saving half an hour and a little personal convenience is too high.

If the availability of comparatively low-price broiler chickens and eggs in the supermarket depends on hanging live birds by their feet from a conveyor belt and letting them bleed to death, or keeping layers crowded in wire chests of drawers and adding orange dye to their feed to disguise the deficiency of their yolks, then the price tag on my frequent consumption of meat protein is too high and I shall have to pay the higher price of free-range poultry and eggs and eat less of them.

If my comfortable habit of a bedtime milk drink is maintained by ruthless, one-sided negotiation with the cocoa producing countries, condemning the farmers to deeper poverty and no education for their children, then the price tag is too high precisely because it is too low. Equal terms of international trade cannot evolve painlessly: we have to become willing to pay more for less because we belong to the same family as the Ghanian cocoa growers.

And if it is argued that the present terms of international trade must be maintained in order to go on offering the enormously high dividends on investments upon which our whole system of pensions and insurance depends, then the price tag on our security is too high. We are compelling the most powerless people in the world to pay a large part of the total cost of it and thereby making it impossible for them to save anything for the future. We are, in fact, stealing security from them.

### Refusing to be conned

Then I would like to offer another slogan which some may prefer as an alternative to the first, while others may add it as a second motto to their escutcheon: *Who are you kidding?*

It needs to be quoted with pride – best of all by a family in unison – every time a television commercial appears on the screen. We must learn to greet with ribald laughter all those patently phoney demonstrations. Samm Sinclair Baker instances a lot of amusing cases from the USA. There was the familiar routine of the woman giving the dirty floor covering a quick wipe-over with some patent cleaner which seemed to clear a magical path through the dirt at one stroke; which was exactly what it did, since the floor had been sprinkled with powdered graphite, and plain water would have done as much. There was the shaving cream advertisement which showed sandpaper being shaved while a silky voice intoned 'Apply, soak – and off in a stroke'. But the 'sandpaper' which was filmed was actually a sheet of transparent plastic to which a layer of sand had been applied. And the ice-cream that didn't melt was actually a vegetable spread normally used for cooking.

*Who are you kidding?* should become our normal response to a great many of the spoken claims of the advertisers as well. Repeating it will at least make us pause long enough to detect the non-statement concealed in the statement. A moment's thought shows that such incontrovertible claims as 'Stay slim with Blank's biscuits', 'Blank keeps you healthier', or 'Blank helps to relieve tension, colds, constipation or whatever' merely invite such questions as 'healthier than what?' and amount to no claims at all. Baker recalls the cartoon caption: 'Seventeen hospitals tested our product and found it completely ineffective, but we can still advertise it as hospital tested.'

Another device which calls for a resounding *Who are you kidding?* is the price-reduction or the bargain offer. Some careful calculation will usually show either that the pence-off price is in fact the normal selling price or that a company selling several different lines is merely losing on the roundabouts in order to attract more custom to the swings. Sometimes the original price is deliberately fixed well above the intended normal selling price in order that, when it is brought down, it can be made to look like a reduction. The advertiser prices the product to retail at £10 and sells it at that price less 40% to the retailer. Then he reduces the retail price to £6·50, less 40% to the retailer. The goods can be labelled. 'Was £10, reduced price £6·50', but actually the new price gives the normal rate of profit to the wholesaler, the retailer and, of course, the advertiser.

But while nurturing such healthy cynicism, we should not let it make us over-confident. The average British housewife is credited with a sturdy price-consciousness that is not easily hoodwinked, yet studies in the supermarkets show that she regularly pays too high a price for many of the most popular products. The advertising experts are very smart operators who know that, even if an advertisement does not persuade a purchaser to buy the particular brand that it recommends, it will increase the sales of the product as a whole – breakfast cereals or washing powders or beer in general. So if the family is going to play the useful game of 'Black List' – marking down for non-purchase everything its members see advertised more than once in a week –

they may have to write off a whole range and not merely the most widely advertised brands. Banning the whole tribe of pre-cooked cereals, for example, in exchange for genuine oatmeal porridge. And if it is food value the family is after, that would not be a bad exchange, even at double the price. Maybe you read about the dietary laboratory where, with sugar and milk added in both cases, the rats that were fed on the brightly coloured cartons thrived better than those that were fed on the breakfast cereals inside the cartons.

Advertising considerably increases the price of the product, not only by adding the fantastic cost of the advertising campaign itself, but even more by persuading the customer to pay more than he need. We ought to be quite clear that that is the aim of a great deal of advertising – not to persuade people to buy the product but to convince them that it is worth paying a higher price for it. There is the in-built snobbery of the small-time status-seeker, as we noticed in the style of appeal that is addressed to the newly-recruited junior typist. But in any highly-pressured consumer society there is a general tendency to equate value with price. Cheapness is almost a liability once the advertisers have got to work making consumers resent the implication that they cannot afford or are not worthy of the best. Working-class women seem more resentful of this low-price image than their middle-class sisters who can afford to be that much less worried about their prestige. Incidentally, a shopping list is an essential weapon in the armoury of the economic underground. Studies in supermarkets and interviews with shoppers reveal that more and more housewives are impulse-buyers. They drift between colourful banks of packages and tins, hypnotized by quantity, lulled by canned music, softened-up at the soft drinks counter, and they buy on impulse. Fewer and fewer are those who arrive with a list of what the household needs, buy it and go. This is what gave the insurance firm of Childs and Wood in Chicago the idea of setting up a counter to sell insurances to passers-by in the department store of Carson Pirie Scott and Company. The experiment was so successful it was established on a permanent basis. Prudence on impulse! – Who are you kidding?

Another kind of buying in which the purchaser may not be considering the price in a fully responsible manner is, of course, hire purchase. The Conservative government of Britain in 1971–3 bent its whole economic strategy towards creating a consumer boom in order to promote domestic investment and restore profits. To achieve this end they encouraged an expansion of consumer credit which increased the hire purchase debt by 27% in twelve months, mainly due to an enormous increase in lending by finance houses. Very few purchasers take the trouble to work out the actual rate of interest they are being required to pay on the credit which the companies advance to them. If they did they would find that it is often as high as 45% – an amount which in other circumstances would be condemned as exorbitant. Careful calculation of mortgage arrangements would often show a similar fleecing of the customer who, in many cases, is a young husband desperate to escape with his wife from the necessity of doubling up with his in-laws. In such situations anger alone is impotent. The exploitation will go on until the developers, the mail-order houses and everyone else who is pitching the price too high are confronted by a determined Christian minority that has learned to shout all together in the name of the Lord of freedom and truth, *Who are you kidding?*

### Travelling light

A third motto I would like to see on the ragged banners of our protest march is *You can't take it with you.* Try that one on the next salesman who draws your wavering attention to the latest BMW masterpiece. The church has always recommended its members to make their daily personal choices in the sober recollection of the fact that none of us will be here for very long. This is only another aspect of that comprehensive frame of reference which we should always take into account when drawing up our budgets and determining our priorities.

But the phrase has more than an eschatological meaning. It is the standing orders of a people on the move. 'You must have your belt fastened, your sandals on your feet and your staff in your hand and you must eat in urgent haste.' So on the eve of Israel's departure from Egypt, the start of their great trek: 'Take nothing for the journey, neither stick nor pack neither bread nor money, nor a second coat.' So Jesus on the eve of his disciple's first mission. Pilgrims travel with packs, not pantechnicons, and revolutionaries allow themselves few commitments.

This suggests that our life-style of protest should always be functional, light-weight and provisional. The best of our modern architects are aware of this. It is bad luck on a great artist like Sir Herbert Baker, for example, that this contemporary mood should have overtaken him so swiftly that most of his spendid designs – India House, South Africa House, New Delhi – look somewhat pretentious now. Since he was commissioned to build so many monuments and memorials, it is not surprising that his churches were monumental too. With what satisfaction he wrote of his cathedral in Cape Town:

> It stands up as the *chevets* of French cathedrals dominate their surroundings, and it is to be hoped that no taller buildings will be allowed to dominate its ascendancy so that it will always be seen as the spiritual centre of the city.

But that is the very spirit which Bishop Dwyer of Reno, who was one of the foremost thinkers on these matters in the United States, castigated most severely.

> The cathedral symbol which has dominated our thinking and imagination for so long, and has dictated the forms and concepts of our building and decoration from actual cathedrals to country parish churches, is dead and had better be buried . . . The cathedral typified wealth and power and esteem, if not downright human pride . . . It was the fortress of faith, the stronghold of religion, the rhetorical assertion of the temporal triumph of Christendom.

Instead of clinging to an ascendancy that no longer exists, the loveliest modern churches on the continent, and a very few in this country, are marked by the austerity and humility of modest proportions, raw concrete and unrendered stone. Some, like Rainer Senn's chapels at Pontarlier and outside Nice, or George Pace's university chapel at Ibadan, actually recall a tent or shelter. Such buildings seem to express a kind of repentance – a repentance that is surely a necessary condition of the church's re-engagement with the world. I hope it will prove to be easier for a future generation of Christians to declare our more recent church buildings redundant and move out of them than it is for us to give up our Gothic heirlooms. We have to design for mobility. We have to design something that looks like the resting-place of the Son of Man.

I have allowed myself this digression into architecture because it symbolizes a change of attitude and even of taste which is going to be essential if our protest against affluence is to succeed. In our homes also we must go for beauty, space, rest and welcome, but not be houseproud. It is better to have no carpet than one we cannot bear to see trodden by dirty shoes – or else we should learn the courtesy of the Japanese and provide slippers for our guests. We must learn to turn a small treat into a celebration. A small community, modelled loosely on the old monastic pattern, with which I shared Easter 1974, celebrated the festival by sharing two boxes of fudge after lunch, and such was the skill of their simplicity, it generated more honest excitement and fun than any expensive self-indulgence could have done. That is the nature of eucharistic living.

The younger generation have a true feeling for the provisional, mobile style – and those who exploit their purchasing power have recognized this and put on the market a phoney poverty of jeans with factory-made patches, handbags and transistor radios in chunky camp-kit designs and costly John the Baptist or Che Guevara hairstyling. We too must beware of phoney simplicity. If our preoccupations are right, if our time and money are thrown into the right struggle, our surroundings will reflect it. There is a kind of bareness, a kind of shabbiness even, which is beautiful because it speaks of beautiful priorities, and all who share the same priorities feel at home in it. This attitude towards property was reflected in great clarity by Daniel Berrigan in an interview which he recorded some time ago. Speaking about the occasion of his original protest against the compulsory draft for the Vietnam war, he said:

> We were trying to say of property that unless it is humanly useful and beautiful, it has no right to exist . . . Yet if in local communities there is a very quiet kind of reintegration of property with human life, that is one kind of subtle thinking and appreciation which makes property beautiful, simple and humanly available.[7]

## Families for defiance

Perhaps you can glimpse now the sort of light-hearted yet deadly serious protest I am proposing as a way of life for our times. Because it is so deadly serious and the pressures are so subtle and, once challenged, so ruthless, we don't stand much chance unless we find ways of living in a corporate opposition. Planning and living in a group gives us the opportunity of talking out the implications of a proposed line of action, speaking as our own devil's advocate among sympathizers, abandoning inadequate reasons in favour of sounder ones, and strengthening each other by affectionate prompting and challenge. The family is the best unit of witness in this matter, and I believe that parents and older children should try to work out for their own home the standards and patterns of a common life which will be a leaven of simplicity and responsibility in the dough of a society that is built on the 'more and more' principle. And if the natural family is sadly incapable of creating any sort of common life, there are man-made 'families' of different kinds which are being formed, often on a provisional basis, for this very purpose. I shall deal with these in the last chapter.

The sort of proposals that such family units should be adopting are these. They should always be undertaken with a sense of humour, for impishness is more likely to survive than grimness against the 'hideous strength' with which we are contending. These are only a few ideas, offered as a model to stimulate others.

'Let's limit our family to one child of our own and one adopted brother or sister.'

'Let's black-list any brand we see advertised more than once in a week, and switch not to a different brand but a different product altogether.'

'No second helpings unless there are guests – though the first can be generous, especially for the kids.'

'Let's take the trouble and expense of searching for natural foods produced naturally – free-range poultry and their eggs, stone-ground wholemeal flour, etc., of which a little does more good.'

'Let's go for quality in other things as well, and make them last even if we have fewer of them. And if something we've liked a lot is broken, let's bear the whole pain of that and not try alleviating it with a quick replacement.'

'No second car. Perhaps not even one. And the next car we buy will be bought to last for its natural life, not to be junked or given in part-exchange after two years.'

'Let's accept the extra effort and expense of using the products of the poorer countries, cane rather than beet sugar, soap rather than detergent. Real cotton and wool rather than man-made fibres.'

'Let's pay cash on the dot every time; no more credit cards or HP. Even the gas bill can be settled by cash transaction at the bank, saving the cost of a cheque.'

'Let's go for new-style hospitality; simple fare and a much wider circle of guests. And let's develop the hospitality of our car also.'

That is enough to begin with. There are a great many other areas of life which we could also bring under the healing touch of the phrase 'enough is enough'.

One of the commissions of the British Council of Churches Church Leaders' Conference in September 1972 produced a short paper containing rather similar questions for consideration by congregations or smaller groups of Christians. I set it out here as a document worthy of study, providing the study leads to action.

## Towards Simplicity of Life

1. *See yourself as a citizen of the planet*
   Questions of poverty and environment are distorted if seen only in local or national terms. (That is a point I have frequently made above.)

2. *Waste-watching*
   Where you have a choice
   resist obsolescence; choose the longer lasting
   support public transport with your feet and your vote
   question advertisement
   resist wasteful packaging.

3. *Question your own life-style – not your neighbour's!*

4. *If possible, work out your way of life with the help of a group (family, friends, congregation)*
   Asking such questions as:
   How can we measure our real needs (by the standards of our neighbours or by the needs of the poor)?
   How can we be joyful without being greedy or flamboyant (eg in hospitality)?
   How far does our personal way of life depend on *society's* wealth? Can our society's way of life be simpler? Is there any such change we ourselves can work for?
   How can we be good stewards without being over-scrupulous? What decisions about personal life are the decisive ones to make (eg budgeting; family size)?
   How can others benefit from what we have (our home, our car and other possessions)?

5. *Points to ponder*
   Happiness is knowing what I can do without
   My greed is another's need
   Am I detached from worldly goods if I keep what I have and want to add to them?[8]

It is not difficult to see that swimming against the tide of an affluent consumer society and defying its pressures is going to entail sacrifice. We must avoid self-dramatization and keep a strong sense of humour. We should not take ourselves too seriously, but should take Christ much more seriously. We badly need the gay devotion of the very first monks, the desert fathers, who staged their dramatic drop-out from a world in which the inflationary consumer society of the later Roman Empire concluded its first official alliance with the formerly outlawed Christian movement and so brought the counter-culture into the establishment itself. Monasticism was the life-style of the protest. And I believe that the impasse of our global economic imbalance calls for a new kind of monastic movement which will be secular, non-celibate and non-institutional.

I would suggest that such a movement must include three elements which I would call simplicity, non-violent techniques and community. Each of these words, as it stands, is open to great misunderstanding. I shall try to explain what I mean by the second and the third in the last two chapters of this book. But first let me make clear what I mean by simplicity.

Human nature as a whole has always been baffled by the peculiarly Christian virtues. At the very beginning St Paul realized that in face of this inveterate incomprehension we have to expect to be fools for Christ's sake. The word 'silly' originally meant blessed, merry, innocent, guileless, holy; but that combination of qualities appeared to ordinary eyes as something fatuous. 'Simple' has undergone the same corruption: to be uncomplicated and single-minded is to be weak-minded in the eyes of the world. And the traditional Christian response to all this is to accept the role of clown with gladness. If we are going to keep the light touch in this grim battle and sustain our sense of humour we must try not to be too reasonable. If it flatters us to be called sensible we are lost already, for rationality is the stock-in-trade of the commercial society, for all its basic madness. 'It is an irrational act,' argued one of the Puritan divines at the time when capitalism was taking wing, 'and therefore not fit for a rational creature, to love anyone farther than reason will allow us.' Just how reasonable was the cross? So I think we should welcome the outrageous and fantastic into our style of life. It will at least serve to keep us and others laughing.

This was typical of those desert fathers with their comical affairs with lions and scorpions and their absurd pillars. It was most typical of St Francis, who loved to pull the leg of another brother just when he was teaching the most startling and profound truth. He more than anyone else taught men to take Christ seriously in such a way as to make it impossible for them to take themselves seriously. Once a poor woman came to the Portiuncula begging for alms. Francis turned to Peter Catani and asked if he had anything they could give her. Peter replied that the only thing in the house was the New Testament from which the lessons were read at matins. 'Give it to her,' cried Francis, 'that she may sell it for her necessity. For I firmly believe that would please the Lord and the Blessed Virgin more than if we were to read in it.' How absurdly spontaneous and how penetratingly right for anyone wanting to keep a new movement of the Spirit free from religiosity. Or again — and I quote now from Bishop Moorman's beautiful study of St Francis:

About the year 1211 Francis and Brother Masseo set off on a journey to France. Having reached a small town, suffering much from hunger, each went to beg for food. Masseo being tall and handsome did well; but Francis being small and insignificant got nothing but a few scraps of dry bread. When they met again by a fountain Francis explained: 'O Brother Masseo, we are not worthy of such vast treasure.' But Masseo protested that this was really absurd when they had so little to eat and no place of their own in which to eat it. But Francis was quite impenitent. 'This it is,' he cried, 'that I account vast treasure, wherein is nothing at all prepared by human hands but whatsoever we have is given by God's own providence . . . the bread that we have begged . . . the table of stone so fine . . . the fount so clear; wherefore I will that we pray unto God that He make us to love with all our heart the treasure of Holy Poverty which is so noble that thereunto did God Himself become a servitor.'[9]

The word 'poverty' has come to sound so negative and extreme in our ears that I prefer the word 'simplicity' because it puts the emphasis on the right point. The involuntary poverty of millions in our time is so degrading and destructive that the vocation of most of us is not to identify ourselves with it – though some are certainly called that way – but to combat the attitudes and actions which cause it. Our enemy is not possessions but excess. Our battle-cry is not 'Nothing!' but 'Enough!' But the defiant simplicity we need is essentially of the same spirit as the poverty which St Francis sought with such ardour. It consists of the ability to do without for the sake of freedom. Only those who are not afraid of being stripped can escape the insidious blackmail of the people whose philosophy is that every man has his price. It is not merely that simplicity and plainness is a price worth paying for freedom, which is certainly true, but that simplicity rightly embraced is itself a precious facet of freedom, and of wisdom too. One of the wiser counsels of Mao Tsetung is to send all his bureaucrats, all his university graduates, back to the villages from time to time to recover the deep wisdom and sense of values of the poorest members of society and to remind them-selves of the real people for whose sakes all planning and all technology exist.

That reference to Mao need not alarm us. If Christians are going to defy the assumptions and the values of the affluent industrialized societies we have to be very sure about the road we have chosen to walk and about our reasons for walking it. And when we find, as we shall, that we are accompanied over a considerable stretch of the road by unexpected travelling-companions, this should neither deflect us nor turn us back. President Julius Nyerere, speaking as a fellow-Christian to the Maryknoll Missionary Order in New York in the autumn of 1970, warned them that this would happen:

It is necessary to recognise, however, that others will also be working to promote social justice; we have no monopoly of virtue . . . It is not necessary to agree with everything a man believes, or says, in order to work with him . . . We accept into the Church those who create and maintain the present political and economic system . . . What right, then, have we to reject those who serve mankind, simply because they refuse to accept the leadership of the Church, or refuse to acknowledge the divinity of Jesus or the existence of God? . . . If God were to ask the wretched of the earth who are their friends, are we so sure that we know their answer?[10]

In his book *Superman and Common Men*, Benjamin R. Barber distinguishes three forces that are working for change in our society, each of them potentially radical in their thrust and each reflecting a different kind of frustration. There is the economic struggle against insecurity in which the poor and underprivileged minorities are seeking for a fairer deal; this struggle is almost as old as history, but Barber points out that 'those fighting other newer and more fashionable wars overlook it'. Then there is the racial struggle against discrimination which often manifests itself in economic terms but aims at justice and recognition rather than mere security. And thirdly there is a revolution of values aimed at liberation from the pressures that dehumanize and distort the true meaning of life. He goes on:

The third revolution is the most elusive: it is abstract though intensely personal, compelling yet without historical roots, profoundly sceptical but demanding nothing less than a new faith . . . It confronts the system with the existential query 'Why?' – rendering irrelevant the customary revolutionary questions 'for whom?' and 'by whose leave?' It does not ask for a greater share of the pie; it asks the reason for eating – and, indeed, it expresses a willingness to abstain until sufficient reasons can be found.[11]

Barber points out that these three movements are failing to arouse the allegiance of the practical majority of people because each is engaged more in a struggle with the other two than with the status quo or its defenders. There is no need for mutual fear and antagonism so long as we are quite clear about the objectives we share and also about the place at which our roads will most certainly diverge. If we know why we choose to laugh at ourselves rather than to take ourselves too seriously, to keep our minds flexible and tolerant rather than to surrender them to any fixed ideology, to put our faith in non-violence rather than ruthlessness, and to know that as soon as a different régime is established we shall again be on the side of the victims and the non-conformists even though they will be our former 'enemies', there will be no need to exaggerate the dangers of infection from walking awhile with those whose ultimate aims are opposed to our own because the means they choose betray such different values. Our own might even prove to be the more contagious faith!

# 5

## Do-it-yourself Development

'Whoever lives there,' thought Alice, 'it'll never do to come upon them *this* size: why, I should frighten them out of their wits!' So she began nibbling at the right-hand bit again, and did not venture to go near the house till she had brought herself down to nine inches high.

*Alice's Adventures in Wonderland*

### The church of the shepherd boy

So far we have been considering what ordinary people in their family units might do to create a resistance movement against the pressures and assumptions of the get-richer society. Christians should, however, go a step further. Once we have started to orientate our family life towards this defiance, we should apply the same principles to our church congregations also.

By taking as our model, for example, the suburban parish which was looking forward to its centenary gift-day as a chance to redecorate the rather shabby interior of its church and re-furnish its sanctuary. Then came Bangladesh: and that church remains shabby, and more truly glorious. Or by copying the young bishop from South-east Asia who was disgusted by the price which London's ecclesiastical suppliers asked for a pectoral cross, and picked up a very nice one for 60p in Carnaby Street!

Let us try to lighten the institutional machinery of our church and recover the sense of the provisional and the spirit of poverty which is so free and so strong. Let us stop trying to keep up with the ecclesiastical Joneses in expensive apparatus and techniques and go for simplicity of means in our mission. So we can't bring home the gospel to the young people without a new stage with theatrical lighting and sound equipment? *Who are you kidding?* If we are to reach the people in the housing estate we must build a new ecumenical church centre? But *you can't take it with you* and they are always on the move, anyway. You can't expect us to raise money for your missionary society unless you tell us a simple success story and guarantee that no funds go to political action. Sorry, *the price tag is too high.*

And in our Christian organizations, when we have freedom to create a pattern of relationships that reflect the gospel, should we not more deliberately defy the economic assumptions that are causing such havoc in our secular life? When at last, after the months of internecine strife, the British government agreed that the coal-miners were a special case of hard and dangerous conditions of work which merited a special wage-increase beyond the normal bounds of Phase 3, the total bill was monstrously inflated by the automatic assumption that all the white-collar workers of the industry must have their wages pushed up too, though none of the reasons which justified this action in the case of the underground workers were operative in their case. For in the world of the unions nothing must upset the rigid lines of wage-differentiation. The distances must remain the same all the way up; which means that for ever and a day we set our faces against a more equal society. But must the church follow suit? Should we not expect Christian institutions to hold down the upper part of their pay structure so that the lower levels may be the first to enjoy the thaw? Such action would truly appear to be part of the life-style of protest.

If a considerable number of the members of a particular congregation care about the witness of their church in regard to this aspect of society, they can find out whether the parish or district council has any endowment or other invested funds and then press upon the parish meeting the question whether such funds should not be invested in local enterprises such as a housing association, that will benefit the community even at a lower rate of return. Alternatively, a congregation that has taken the trouble to arm itself with the facts can influence its own ratepayers' association to challenge as socially irresponsible the investment portfolio of the borough council or its lack of concern for the environment. In other words, a mutually supportive congregation of this kind can exercise to the full the democratic potential of responsible citizenship.

For far too long we have been cajoled into thinking of the church as an institution. Of course it *is* an institution and is bound to have a certain institutional structure. But if the church is ever to recover the outlook and attitudes of a mission, its members must steadfastly refuse to be cast in the role of an institution among other institutions, a power-structure among power-structures. That is the image the press always has in mind when it announces 'church withdraws investments' or 'church supports Population Year'. But we know that in its essence the church is not an institution but a movement and, therefore, it is important for us all to study the secrets of rejuvenation by which a well-established institution can retain enough of the sap of vitality to be able to maintain momentum and mobility. Thinking about the processes of institutionalism one can identify six simple rules for ensuring that the main characteristics of a movement are not lost. These are:

Keep the aim limited
Keep the organization small
Cherish the weakness of limited means
Distribute functions widely
Trust local teams with full responsibility
Foster new growth on the fringes

It will be evident from this that I do not put my faith in the big battalions. I distrust the pedlars of an over-all strategy and I despair of the busy housemaids of the church endlessly tidying up its inconsistencies. The great ecclesiastical centralizers, like King Saul of old, put their trust in heavy accoutrements and expensive weapons. He could not bear to see the shepherd boy

87

going unarmed into the contest with Goliath, and almost smothered him in an excess of equipment. But David knew better.

## Enough for what?

The story of David reminds me of a passage in a lecture on ecology given by Professor Charles Birch of Australia a few years ago.

> Originally a unit of population was simply a human being whose needs were met by eating 2,500 calories and 60 grams of protein a day. Man's daily need of energy was equivalent to the continuous burning of a single 100 watt bulb. A unit of population today *in the developed world* consists of a human being wrapped in tons of steel, copper, aluminium, lead, tin, zinc and plastics, each day gobbling up 60 lbs of raw steel and many pounds of other minerals. Far from getting these things in his homeland he ranges abroad much as a hunter and more often than not in the poorer countries. His energy need instead of being equivalent to a single 100 watt lamp is equivalent to ten 1,000 watt radiators continuously burning.[1]

It is hardly surprising that the more thoughtful leaders in the Asian, African, Latin American and Island countries are dubious about the value, let alone the possibility, of emulating such a load of hardware. Hitherto a great part of the 'aid' made available by the rich industrialized nations to those that are poorer has been given on the assumption that they need to become just as industrialized as we are. Yet Africa has been called 'the grave-yard of the tractors' because farmers whose annual income is usually less than £200 have neither the skill nor the heart to keep in good running order a piece of heavy machinery costing £1,500.

One of the earliest critics of the pattern of overseas aid the rich countries are giving to the poorer ones was Dr E. F. Schumacher. Having worked on a report for the Indian Planning Commission in 1963, he began to argue at a conference on rural industrialization held at Cambridge the following year that development aid usually by-passed the rural areas of the poor countries, although they are the areas of greatest need and also the areas on which, in the long run, the economies of the poor countries depend. Unless this rural poverty is tackled at source it is bound to lead to mass migration to the cities and the destructive unrest of a hungry urban proletariat. The most effective aid, therefore, is that which is given in simple ways and on a modest scale to enable innumerable peasants and half-skilled city workers to advance themselves a little at a time. Dr Schumacher described in the May 1969 issue of *Crucible* a textile factory in East Africa, the gift of a European government, which was so highly automated that it needed to employ 500 workers only. The capital value of that plant was about £1½ million, so each work-place had in fact cost £3,000. Yet armed guards were protecting the factory gates from the crowd of young Africans outside who were desperate for jobs. The government of the receiving country had in fact asked for the factory to be built in that far-off rural town because there was so much unemployment in the region. What kind of answer is a plant which employs so few to the massive employment problems of a struggling country?

In contrast to such cynical irrelevance, the Intermediate Technology Development Group has been undertaking much needed research in order to discover, and then to offer, the modest advance and simple improvement which can make all the difference between destitution and progress for millions of small-time farmers, craftsmen, housewives and artisans, and which they themselves will be capable of making and managing. The group has coined the motto: 'Not a hand-out, but a leg-up.'

As a result of the group's contact with universities and technical colleges, two engineering students at Manchester University have recently been permitted to include as a formal part of their degree studies the design of a fool-proof water-raising pump which rural workers in developing countries can make out of local materials, and of a simple lathe which can be used to make it. Another team connected with the group, with the help of Reading University, has designed a machine that can be operated by local labour to manufacture strong, convenient egg-trays for

89

Zambia's poultry farmers, by pulping ordinary waste paper. Not only is the machine itself cheap and easy to run, but any design previously on the market would have had to produce one million egg-trays per month in order to be economic, whereas Zambia's farmers needed only one million per year. Enough was enough.

The Intermediate Technology Development Group in Britain is composed of people from the professions, industry and administration, all of whom have worked overseas. The group has set up panels dealing with industry, textiles, building, agriculture, food, health, water, power, chemistry and the running of different types of co-operatives, and their work has begun to show impressive results. At the beginning of 1974 Germany announced that she will establish an Institute of Intermediate Technology as her contribution to overseas aid in the coming years. Both organizations run on a budget whose modesty compares startlingly with some of the prestige projects which have been dumped into developing countries in the name of 'aid'.

Dr G-C. M. Mutiso, a lecturer in the Department of Government of the University of Nairobi, speaking at a consortium on science, technology and the future of man and society in 1972, offered several examples of how African technologists might employ their resourcefulness in ways that are far more applicable to the African situation than they have hitherto used.

> I am convinced that at the moment we have enough food to feed our population, yet we cannot get it to our people. We have been sold on transportation systems based on the car, the train, and the aeroplane, which serve less than $\frac{1}{3}$ of our populations. We could borrow new durable materials from aeroplane technology and create cheap, new mechanical mules which do not carry as much as Kaduna trucks but which can carry a rural farmer's goods to market over ordinary terrain. Thus we could do without the tarmac roads. In the cities high-speed public transit systems could replace the cars with considerable saving to society. There are viable alternatives if only we have the imagination always to ask: does the technology we are borrowing serve the greatest number of our people at the least cost to the society?[2]

One reads, therefore, with a growing sense of excitement the reports of the Intermediate Technology Development Group describing the invention and production of hand-operated presses for making building blocks out of local soil mixed with 4% cement. One to three men can operate the press successfully, and an eight- to ten-man crew allows continuous use of the machine, digging, mixing and stacking the new blocks. Another creative piece of work was the design of a locally built single-row rice seeder. This, however, emerged from a research project with a much more ambitious aim, namely to identify the worst bottle-necks and labour-shortage peaks throughout the cycle of traditional African agriculture in order that it may be eased at those points by the application of improved techniques without disrupting the old system, only to find that there is nothing to replace it. This is mechanization of a kind that really serves, and does not enslave, the human factor. In Swaziland, where water-supply is a perennial problem, they have designed and built new water-catchment tanks a storage tank holding 50,000 gallons surrounded by a sloping apron of cement which catches the rainfall.

One of the most imaginative development workers I have met in Asia was an elderly Swiss, a man of very few words, who moved in a desultory way on foot or on the public buses from one small town to another, and as his observant eye fell on one poor struggling person after another, he would ask them the question: What would you do with a loan of £10? He found that almost everyone had a private dream. The man selling a dozen tangerines on the pavement dreamed of a fruit-barrow. The knife-grinder would invest in enough equipment to set up as a small-time barber. And so, if his intuitive judgment of people gave assent, this man would lend the £10. And after years of acting in this way he could recall only three cases in which the loan had not eventually been repaid in full. This is the way to enlist in a nation's development programme the immense hidden reserve of effort and ingenuity that is locked up in the small entrepreneurs. The potential and the invincible optimism of all these myriads of little people is most movingly voiced in a paper produced by the village committee of an almost unknown place in Botswana where people, in consultation with a local school, are experimenting with many possible new industries that could be started at low cost.

> We must now learn how to progress and develop without money . . . We must remind ourselves how to make things from the materials around us . . . For example, we must learn how to take the white limestone and to burn it with wood so that we can make from it lime for building. We must all learn how to make bricks and to burn them with wood in kilns so that they become hard. If we crush the bricks and mix the brick dust with lime we get a sort of cement . . . We can make doors and doorframes from our own timber, and we can even make glass by melting bottles in furnaces. We can make windmills for our wells. We can all learn to thatch. All of us can learn improved methods of gardening using very little water, and we can produce a great variety of vegetables. We can increase production of eggs by crossing our fowls with imported cocks. We can introduce new rams to cross with our goats to increase milk production and also to produce mohair which is like wool . . . We can grow sunflower and groundnuts to produce cooking oil, and cotton from which we can make rough cloth . . . we can learn to tan by new methods and so learn to make leather. We can also obtain fat from which to make soap, candles and polish. It is not difficult to learn to spin wool and cotton and to learn to weave or knit either, into blankets, jerseys or socks. Most of us are too poor to do any of these things by ourselves. We can solve our problems by working together, helping each other . . . If we work together in this way, we will find that each one has work and that we shall be able to obtain by working together most of those things we want to buy from the shops but cannot because we have no money.[3]

Fragile hope, heartbreakingly unlikely to succeed; yet of such is the kingdom of the future. This kind of development calls for the modesty and naturalness of people helping people. Unfortunately that is the form of aid that the rich industrial nations seem least eager to offer. As Dr Schumacher wrote two years ago:

> Astonishingly, the aid-givers simply assume that *they* have the appropriate knowledge to help the poor: they think they know and therefore rush straight into 'projects'. But what makes them think that they know how to bring help to destitute villages, when they have no such villages in their own countries? What makes them think that they can teach poor people how to use their labour power with virtually no

capital, when the entire experience and education of these experts derives from societies where labour is secure and capital plentiful?[4]

The instance I have already quoted of the machine that produced far more egg-trays than Zambia's farmers needed raises all the questions and all the arguments with which this book is trying to deal. Why shouldn't Zambia steal a march and manufacture 12 million trays a year to sell to the surrounding countries? But, on the other hand, why should she, when their problem, like hers, is inadequate employment and inadequate use of local resources? 'Economics', says Dr Schumacher, 'does not start with goods; it starts with people and their education, organization and discipline.' Not goods, but people. That is the true rationale of the theology of enough. 'Enough is enough' is a fine standard of measurement, but it begs the question: enough for what? The answer is: enough for the personal. The question each of us has to ask time after time, corporately as well as individually, is this: will this purchase, this change, these plans, these investments, make our relationships more fully human in the context of our one human family and of our one inter-related world? Will this enrich or impoverish the personal value of other people? Will it clarify or cloud man's recognition of himself as the child of God? Do we still dare to ask such questions?

## Use all gently

The title 'Intermediate Technology' points to a scale that is somewhere between the traditionally evolved technology of the hoe, the hand-loom or the cart and the sophisticated industrialized technology of the combine harvester, the textile factory or the jet-engine. Intermediate technology has the immediate effect of enlarging rather than diminishing the human beings whose strength and skill it augments. It fits into their scheme of things, their system, without toppling it off balance and so destroying it. And, above all, it deals gently with the environment.

This may sound like sentiment; but I would remind you of the violence of our industrialized methods of cutting a new motorway through the landscape, spraying fertilizer from the air, eliminating the rabbit population or holding back the seas. I am not now saying that any of these uses of science are inherently wrong in themselves, but they generate in their users an aggressive wilfulness that cannot tolerate resistance. The very violence of our technology is an operative element in the excess which mars our civilization. After his long years of brooding in many different fields of knowledge, Albert Schweitzer put his finger on this arrogant ruthlessness towards whatever gets in our way as the fatal flaw in our culture and offered his concept of 'reverence for life' as the only way to recover a stable world-view. 'Gentle' is another word whose meaning has been somewhat degraded: it originally meant behaving as a member of the family and therefore observing the relationships of courtesy. It was particularly expected of a family that enjoyed privilege and had no excuse for throwing its weight about. The creation has the right to expect such courtesy from the children of God and, so St Paul says, still waits with eager expectation for those whose family likeness will be apparent. That is why, basically, true technology should be gentle.

The good sense of that principle surely becomes apparent when one considers the list of countries, all of them with a predominantly rural economy, in which the industrialized powers have set out to train local scientists in nuclear technology. Since 1959 research reactors have been established in the Congo (Kinshasha), Venezuela, Taiwan, Portugal, Thailand, Turkey, South Korea, Vietnam, Iran, Indonesia and Columbia. By what sinister arithmetic can projects of such an outrageous expense be counted as an asset to a community that is struggling to secure a better living standard for its people? Leonard Beaton, who revealed these facts in his book *Must the Bomb Spread?*, remarked that 'only a social psychologist could hope to explain why the possessors of the most terrible weapons in history should have sought to spread the necessary industry to produce them in the belief that this could make the world safer'.[5]

Or, as another example of the stupid violence of our solutions to comparatively simple problems, consider the case of a small African community growing sugar-cane. It all has to be transported to a sugar factory many miles away at a cost which reduces the growers' cash return to a minimum. They are then expected to buy their own sugar at 8p per pound. Forty years ago, or so, the cultivators owned some simple equipment to turn their cane into sugar for their own use. But this has been replaced by highly sophisticated machinery which is totally beyond their financial means. The simple equipment which served them so much better in the past is unobtainable today. But which is the gentler and truer technology: the far-off factory paying dividends to its shareholders or the intermediate technology worker who is prepared to design and make a similar piece of simple equipment to that which they used formerly? To quote Dr Schumacher again:

> But time is short, and 'helping them to help themselves' should not be delayed by a single day. In most cases, it is the small cultivator or farmer whose need is the most urgent, and it is a need for help beyond his purely agricultural activities. If he could but store his products effectively and safely, it might enable him to avoid crop losses of 30% or even more. If he could but take his products through the first stages of processing before he attempted to sell them, this would absorb surplus labour and greatly enhance his cash income. If he could make some use of his agricultural waste products, and manufacture locally only a few of the goods which he now has to buy from the town (although, in many cases, they used to be made in the village a generation ago), this again would help employment and welfare. To make headway along any of these lines, not to speak of local manufactures from *other* than local raw materials, such as making simple tools and implements from imported iron and steel, he needs, above all, technological help, because the equipment he has got himself, or can make by traditional methods, is too primitive to be viable, and the equipment he might buy from modern industry is too sophisticated and too expensive for him.[6]

### Prosper thou the work of our hands

In the village of Otterthotti in India one Catholic missionary has been able to transform the outlook and aspirations of the whole community because he knew how to enlist the help of the local people to bring about the small-scale changes which were the key to the whole situation. The way to any lasting development seemed to be blocked by the stranglehold of the landowners and moneylenders upon the poorest labouring caste. When he received his first grants through Oxfam, Father Godest recruited his labour gangs for the construction of dams and the deepening of wells from among these landless workers, thus releasing them from the grip of the money-lender landowners. He also set up village co-operatives to provide fertilizers, improved hybrid seeds and, if need be, cash. So, to the great rage of the landowners, the helpless began to help themselves. Richard Exley, describing the new spirit of this village, said:

> It was intriguing to see that virtually everything the people used they made themselves, either in Otterthotti or in neighbouring villages. Their ploughs were made at smithy level, with wood culled from the forest and iron heated on the charcoal fire. Their simple earthenware pots are turned on the potter's wheel, hand-turned. Their baskets and grain containers were woven by the basket maker, using local bamboo. Even their brass pots are sometimes hand-beaten.[7]

The reference to village co-operatives in that story reminds me of a very important function of savings banks and credit unions. The Credit Union movement, which was born over a hundred years ago in Germany, has proved to be one of the most stimu-lating forms of co-operative activity. This is because it is im-mediately apparent to each member that the more he puts into it the more he can get out of it. He is only lent what the com-munity knows he has the capacity to repay. A Credit Union is an institution created and controlled by the people themselves. A small group of church leaders in Kampala have in the past few years been trying to solve the problem of urban poverty and unemployment. They persuaded the Church Board of Finance to invest £2,500 in a small poultry farm on land just outside the city boundaries. They opened savings clubs and a credit bank and provided training courses so that those with no experience of these things could understand how to take advantage of them.

They established a Housing Association to develop housing for low income groups. Advancing from this solid financial platform they went on to create two small worker-owned factories, one for food processing and canning, the other a leather factory. Every worker has a share in the responsibility and realizes that he is participating in the demonstration of a Christian alternative to the present industrial structures whereby the rich grow richer and the workers receive only a grudging wage.

In his address to the Maryknoll Missionary Order which I have already quoted, Julius Nyerere insisted that all men who are suffering from poverty, whether in the under-developed or in the industrialized societies, need above everything else to be helped to stretch themselves. They need to be given confidence in their ability to take control of their own lives. And the church, he said, must give up working *for* such people, and start working *with* them. This has for some years been the message of the Christian Medical Commission of the World Council of Churches. The 100-bed hospital begins to look more and more like that distant sugar-factory which, for all its greater efficiency, turns out to be the great inhibitor of local advance. Such places – factories or hospitals – serve to emphasize the absolute distinction between those who have gained the hidden knowledge – the *cognoscenti* – and the rest of us who depend upon them.

Dr Bob Lambourne, who burned out his life in the service of this particular ideal, told of an area in Africa, served for 50 years by a famous pediatric hospital, where the infant mortality rate had remained at a steady 282 per thousand. The children were dying of malaria, dysentery and untended sores. Each of these three killers could have been almost eliminated by a programme of community training in preventive health. And the child victims of these diseases could have been cured by a simple examination and a course of tablets. A new doctor decided to abandon the idolatry of excellence which he had learned in his training school and take a few 15-year-old girls from the local school, teach them and send them into the villages. They made many mistakes, some of them disastrous from the traditional

97

medical point of view. Fortunately there was not a legal system
that could sue for wrong diagnosis! But in five years the infant
mortality rate dropped to 78 per thousand. What had been
killing all those children before was a sacred cow of professional-
ism.

### The tyranny of the packaged export

Julius Nyerere's Arusha Declaration, with its passionate deter-
mination to eliminate the master-servant differentials from
society, is very wary of foreign investment and industrialization.
It says:

> Big hospitals are in towns, and they benefit only a small section of the
> people of Tanzania. Yet if we have built them with loans from outside
> Tanzania, it is the overseas sale of the peasant's produce which provides
> the foreign exchange for repayment. Those who do not get the benefit
> of the hospitals must carry the major responsibility for paying for
> them.[8]

This basic imbalance between the fortunate minority that
benefits from most forms of Western 'aid' and the unfortunate
majority whose labour has to repay the loans, is very trenchantly
argued in an article by Ivan Illich:

> Traffic jams develop in São Paolo while almost a million North-
> Eastern Brazilians flee the drought by walking five hundred miles.
> Latin American doctors get training at The Hospital for Special
> Surgery in New York, which they apply to only a few, while amoebic
> dysentery remains endemic in slums where 90 percent of the popula-
> tion live . . . Each car which Brazil puts on the road denies fifty people
> good transportation by bus. Each merchandised refrigerator reduces
> the chance of building a community freezer. Every dollar spent in
> Latin America on doctors and hospitals costs a hundred lives . . . Had
> each dollar been spent on providing safe drinking water, a hundred
> lives could have been saved.[9]

So high-powered advertising, tough trade-negotiations and
political pressure compel the governments of poor countries to
spend their resources on the pre-packaged exports which the
industrialized countries deem to be good for them instead of on

the more appropriate amenities which could benefit the mass of their people. Very few of such sophisticated, expensive bits of technology have been specially adapted to the conditions or economies of the poorer countries; their pattern is dictated by the convenience and profit of the exporters. It comes as something of a shock to discover that Ivan Illich includes the examination-oriented pattern of primary and secondary schooling among the pre-packaged exports of the industrial nations. All the poor countries spend upwards of eighteen per cent of their tax-derived public income on this universally-accepted pattern of schooling. Like the airports, air-conditioned hotels and hospitals, this school-system benefits the few who get through all the bottle-necks into the universities at the expense of the many who, as Ivan Illich says, 'before dropping out, have been taught that those who stay longer have earned the right to more power, wealth and prestige'. Tens of thousands of school drop-outs flood the inadequate labour markets of all the poor countries, and more lasting than any other lessons they may have learned in their classrooms is the knowledge of their inadequacy and failure. The fortunate few, on the other hand, who have gone right through the educational process, have emerged with a different lesson stamped indelibly on their minds: they have learned the appetites and ambitions of a consumer society, and the things they want to buy are the exports of the industrialized nations.

Of course that is not the whole story, and it would be grossly unjust to thousands of deeply dedicated schoolteachers in the poorer countries not to recognize the many individual pupils whose minds they have awakened to new worlds of awareness and delight. But these are the occasional rewards of conscious effort; those other more poisonous lessons have been imbibed unwittingly from the system itself, and by the great majority.

Intermediate technology is discovering a host of healthier alternatives to the package-deal solutions to the problems of development. It will be much harder to discover valid alterna-tives to 'school' as we understand it. Ivan Illich, Paulo Freire and others are asking whether the process of formal education need be confined to the years of childhood. At present the Latin American countries provide each child with, on average, anything between eight and thirty months of continuous class attendance; there might, however, be many advantages in making one or two months a year obligatory for all citizens below the age of thirty. It has been shown that an adult can be taught to read in one-tenth the time and for one-tenth the cost it takes to teach a child, and even while he is being taught he can begin to teach someone else. Or again, if the pitiful amount that a poor nation can spend on public education were used to provide every child in the country with the basic supply of books, pictures, coloured blocks and counting games which are usually totally absent from the homes of the poor, might this not contribute far more to the progress of true education in a country? Only experiment and research can answer these questions, and what more creative contribution could anyone make to the kingdom of right relationships than that?

Those who are already dedicated to intermediate technology know well enough that whoever undertakes this 'counter-research' must begin by doubting what is obvious to everyone else. Then he must persuade or press those who have the power of decision to act against their own short-term interests. And then he must manage to survive among people who think he is out to destroy the very foundations of their world. Yet survive he must. Ivan Illich writes:

> The only way to reverse the disastrous trend to increasing under-development, hard as it is, is to learn to laugh at accepted solutions in order to change the demands which make them necessary. Only free men can change their minds and be surprised.[10]

So once again we find that we are on the side of laughter, the laughter of little David splashing across the brook towards Goliath. But laughter in solitude turns bitter as it grows insecure; for lasting mirth we need the company of others. And that is the topic of my last chapter.

# 6

## *Cells of Dissent*

'Who cares for *you*?' said Alice (she had grown to her full size by this time). 'You're nothing but a pack of cards!'

*Alice's Adventures in Wonderland*

### *United we stand*

In view of all that has been said, it is not surprising that an enormous number of people of all ages and in many different countries have come to the conclusion that unless we can discover a radically new style of living, and can put it into practice, the delicate balance of life on this planet will be irretrievably deranged and we shall be plunged into chaos. The threat of this situation impinges upon us both from the outside and from the inside. In the world around us we see the disparity between wealth and poverty growing worse, not better; the environmental and population crises mounting towards the point of no return; and the unbridled economy of growth devouring more and more of the world's irreplaceable resources. And in the world within us the stress of tension, loneliness, guilt and futility pushes us towards the brink of breakdown. It has been said that we are living in two deserts – an exploited planet and a soul in agony – which are in truth one desert. And the recognition of these things is compelling more and more of us to make the great refusal and insist on living by some alternative values. And then we find, to our utmost dismay, that a lonely recantation is little more than a gesture. One man's 'Count me out' sounds very much like 'Stop the world, I want to get off'. And the voice of hard-headed materialism is quick to cry 'Escapist!'

And so for the steadying of resolve and the earthing of idealism more and more people are finding ways of uniting for resistance. Some are pessimistic and have no greater hope than to salvage a few years of sanity and peace while the world rolls on to ruin. Others, more positive or perhaps more activist, believe that such groups can be set up as models of an alternative way, signs of the kingdom of right relationships.

I believe we should follow with far more serious interest this movement of exploration in the direction of new man-made families and fellowships. It is far larger than most people imagine. In 1969 it was estimated that there were more than 500 communal ventures in the United States with a total membership of over 10,000. More than four per cent of the Jewish population in Israel is living in *kibbutzim* – about 235 different communal settlements. There are about 50 communes in Japan, some of them consisting of over 200 persons. In Holland there are probably about 200 community experiments run by members of the Roman Catholic Church. In Britain the number is probably considerably smaller. More and more of the young, and also the not-so-young – the married couples and those in the early years of a job – are choosing to rent or buy large run-down houses and combine to form a kind of extended family in order that they and their children may enjoy the dynamics of an integrated affectionate group to help one another in their defiance of the conventional expectations of society. But this conscious idealism ought to be seen in the context of a much wider spread of shared living which is motivated simply by convenience and the new gregariousness of the younger generation. Students and young workers prefer the makeshift freedom of shared premises to the vigilant attentions of a landlady. Many of the 'settlements', sponsored around the turn of the century by Oxbridge colleges and other philanthropic benefactors as centres of social service and club work in the poorer working-class areas of our larger cities, are finding a new function in these days as low-rent communal hostels for 'residents' who go out to work. We should bear in mind this wider background of changing social habits when we try to weigh the significance of what can properly be called the commune movement.

I drew a distinction just now between those who are seeking an alternative life-style with a positive hope of changing the trends in society before it is too late and those who have no such hope but think they have found an oasis in the desert. Andrew Rigby, Lecturer in Sociology at Aberdeen, makes some more precise distinctions in his study of communes, *Alternative Realities*. He calls the more hopeful ones who are still concerned to bring about radical changes in society, the activist type. Among the more disillusioned seekers who hope for no more than their personal fulfilment, he distinguishes two types: the freedom-seekers who want to escape from the constraints of a more conventional world, and the security-seekers who want to belong to a supportive group that will alleviate their feelings of estrangement or loss of identity. Within those categories Rigby makes further sub-divisions which are very discerning but which I cannot pursue now.

### Man-made families

This sort of analysis is a great help towards understanding, but in practice it is not so easy to label any particular commune. A small group in Norfolk, for example, calling itself the Shrubb Family, believes that it is 'trying to do something positive about some of modern society's ailments', yet finds its attention is increasingly focused on the quality of its own community life and the problems that arise from it. Though still quite small, this commune has been established for four years and had a collective title to the house and land. I quote from Richard Shrubb, who kindly wrote for me a long account of the developments this group had experienced.

We used to have a lot of rules and regulations about economic structure, responsibilities and commitments, but the general pattern seems to be that more and more of them get discarded as time goes by because they cease to be important . . . Everyone puts everything they earn into the common pool, so income becomes a joint effort which really keeps us working together. If it was a scene where everyone puts in so much money each week it would be too restricting for the sort of people that we are, and we want more involvement with each other than that would allow. Even the pooling of income is not rigidly observed; Christine gets Social Security for her and her son Rufus, and as she's here half-time and half-time with the Global Village Trucking Company's commune close by she works it all out and we are happy she's here when she wants to be. So if rules and regulations cease to be important, what is it that is? We think it's the feeling, the love, the vibration, whatever you call it; it's that part that's the spirit of the place and the people that live here. If it's positive energy flowing freely out, then nothing else seems to be a hassle; but if it's negative and fragmented it drags everyone down into petty arguments and friction . . .

Apart from housework and looking after the goats, there's the garden which always demands a lot of time. At the moment we are getting together some horse-drawn vehicles as an alternative to motor-power and it's really rewarding work. We don't have a good workshop but we've started work on one where some old sheds have fallen down. Thanks to Roy Cutler and friends (Commune Services), we are just about ready to dig out the foundations. Anyone who wants to come and help us is more than welcome. Visitors are never turned away, although we prefer people to write first. Some people fit in straight away and others don't; I think shy people find it a bit difficult. We don't have much privacy here and that upsets a few who aren't used to sharing a bathroom and loo, but it becomes a necessity with a lot of people using the same facilities. We're all built basically the same, so what are we hiding anyway?

We don't have a bank account any more, because we don't want our money invested by them into something we wouldn't put it into ourselves. Everything we need seems to come to us at the right time, which gives us a lot of faith in what we are doing.

He goes on to express delight that they are on such good terms with their neighbours and participate in the local pub, church and Women's Institute operatic group. They are also very closely linked with at least two other communes in Norfolk, and feel that in common with them they are registering their protest and demonstrating an alternative way. They have not yet resolved, however, the question of an agreed internal discipline with regard to members who seem to shirk their share of the work, especially in an emergency.

The Selene Community, though always small and suffering from a rapid turnover, has given great impetus to the whole movement by duplicating a bi-monthly journal. In that respect the members are consciously fostering the spread of an alternative society. So it is surprising to find that the life-style of Selene itself is so introverted and esoteric. Their home is a very derelict farm property in Carmarthenshire and, besides occasional experiments with group marriage, they pursue a revival of nature-paganism.

> Selene welcomes members of other inclinations, of sentiments different from our own, and on terms which in large measure you yourselves will define, for we feel the need of community is urgent, the need to co-operate, to create a liveable environment and grow our own food and make our clothes before we all succumb to the Monolith . . . But we're not turning away from the Moon Maiden. Our fellow communards after the day's work might want to listen to music, or read, or engage in talk or quiet or love. Then we will choose our peace: we will go out into the wild places and speak to the Moon Maiden and hear her song.

Entirely different in intention are the communes that consist of several middle-class families who find that by pooling their resources and undertaking certain chores jointly, they can afford a standard of gracious living which would be beyond their means separately. Postlip Hall, an Elizabethan manor house near Winchcombe, is a good example of this pragmatic clubbing which has very little to do with resisting the status quo.

Another kind of man-made family with a clearly therapeutic intention are the Simon and Cyrenian Communities which have been established in several different places in Britain. These have come into being in order to offer a non-judgmental, healing community which can receive people who are suffering from various mental and personality disorders – vagrants, addicts or other particularly vulnerable people.

Many communes, particularly the smaller ones in the cities, regard their shared home more as a means than an end in itself; it is the headquarters from which they engage in active political effort to bring about radical change in the ways of the world. This pattern is, on the whole, more common on the continent of Europe.

*Alternative Realities* reveals a sharp distinction between those who join a commune out of disillusionment over the possibility of changing society by political action (demonstrations, lobbys, sit-ins, propaganda) and those who regard their commune as a base for concerted action and a model to show the rest of society a practical way of life built on different assumptions and values. Rigby quotes a member of one such group as saying:

> I don't think you can remould society by taking it en bloc. But one can do so, I think, by setting up lots of little examples. If they are good, people will follow them, if not and they don't, well they don't deserve to be followed.[1]

He describes a small commune which existed for a short time in Blackheath. The curate of a local parish and his wife shared a large detached house with one other woman and five more men, including another clergyman. As a group they tried to involve themselves in local community action. They achieved very little, in fact, partly because the only house they had been able to come by was situated in an area of middle-class house owners who, according to Rigby, 'were quite capable of making their demands heard if they had a mind to do so' and when they turned their attention to the working-class housing estates nearby they were viewed as an interfering body of long-haired students. So they tended to give up group action in favour of individual efforts, and these were more and more diverted into anti-South African protest, that familiar whipping-boy of those who have failed to find a relevant local objective. While they stayed together the eight pooled their income and set aside ten per cent to finance their political activities. The one married couple found they were more and more left with the running of the household while the others enjoyed the irresponsibility of dependents. This dependency syndrome seems to threaten any residential community with a programme of social and political action; they tend to pick up the victims of the social problems they are trying to combat (the unhoused, the inadequate, youngsters on probation, etc.) until all their energies are diverted from challenging society to caring for individuals.

Yet, in spite of the pitfalls, solid victories can be won by a group with a strong corporate identity and a limited target. It was out of a small determined group in Holland that a body called the Angolan Committee was brought into being early in 1972 to campaign to get Angolan coffee banned from the Dutch market. This was because most of the output of this fourth largest coffee-producing country was being grown, according to an official United Nations report under 'a brutal system of compulsory labour'. First the Angolan Committee published a carefully documented book revealing the labour practices in the plantations. Then they approached the management of all the main coffee roasters in Holland. One of these agreed to support the boycott and this in turn persuaded the Social Democratic Labour party to back it. Next the municipal council of Rotterdam and three of the trade unions announced their support. The remaining roasting firms capitulated and Angolan coffee had been effectively banned from the valuable Dutch market.

It is in such ways that human conscience can be freed from despair and small local groups encouraged to believe that their struggle for more humane and responsible relationships need not be in vain.

### Signs of another way

So far I have touched on the commune and residential group movement in general. The growth of specifically Christian cells and communes is only a small part of this, but it has great significance for anyone who is concerned about the relevance of the church to the human condition in our day. Moreover, because the Christian minority in this movement has its roots in the long tradition of Western monasticism, it has some well proved insights to contribute to strengthen the movement as a whole. In New York and Chicago, Brothers of Taizé who are sharing community life with Roman Catholic Franciscans have told me that members of purely secular or Buddhist-oriented communes often approach them, recognizing a family likeness but asking how it is they manage to stay together year after year while their own groups are so transient.

For the past thirty years and more there have been many experiments in new forms of Christian community, experiments that dispense with life vows, include men and women and family units as well as single people. The Bruderhof movement, the Catholic Action Institutes, the Iona Community, St Julian's Community, Lee Abbey and Scargill, the Taizé Community and that at Grandchamps, the Ecumenical Sisterhood of Mary in Germany and the Evangelical Academies, the Grail, the groups calling themselves L'Arche, the Servants of Christ the King, the Foculari – one could go on and on. I can only select a few for fuller description in order to show the great range of possibilities.

The Ashram Community was founded, mainly by Methodists, in 1967. At present it has slightly less than one hundred members. Its members are committed to a dogged loyalty to the established church structures but see the need for new forms of fellowship, worship and action in the world. The figure of Jesus is the focus of their devotion and the model of their life style. They are trying to develop a more 'affective' and therefore less dogmatic relationship to Jesus as the source of their understanding of themselves and the world. So far there are two 'community houses', each with about eight members. Those who live in them are clear that they want to become a para-church with their own experimental worship, their own forms of evangelism and their own responsibility to one another and to the surrounding community. They maintain a communal fund. The majority of the members of the Ashram Community, however, continue to live in their own milieu, but commit themselves to keep in touch with one another by attending residential conferences twice a year, and meeting other members in a locality more frequently, either for a day at a time or at regular evening meetings as a cell-group. Members pay either one per cent of their income or £2 annually to the Ashram fund besides making a 'day's pay' contribution to some cause agreed by the community as a whole. All are pledged to seek a modest style of life relevant to a world of poverty and consciously combating the pressures of the affluent culture. This 'family', which is one of the most stable of the recent experiments, is written up very effectively by John Vincent in a small book called *The Jesus Thing*.

A similarly modest movement is 'Life-Style', founded by Horace Dammers, Dean of Bristol, in 1971. This is not a residential community but a fellowship of individuals who want to bind themselves to some personal rule that reflects concern for the environment and the conservation of the earth's resources and a more just sharing between nations.

The Roadrunners at Chorlton, Manchester, is a commune in the full sense of the word. Founded by four Christian students in 1971 it was closely linked for the purpose of political action with the local Community Research Action Group. They have tried to make a family-like structure with an atmosphere of acceptance and care. Visitors and people in need of human support of any kind are encouraged to drop in and help with the chores. An account in the journal *Community* says:

> One marked example of this is perhaps a lonely and rather nervous old man who now feels that he is quite welcome just to call and sit down and play the piano, so long as this is not causing anyone annoyance, whether the people who originally made contact with him are there or not . . . Trivial arguments tended not to happen so much as they did in the small close-knit family units that we were used to because these sorts of quarrels can be embarrassing when played out in front of a number of people.[2]

They go in for simple trades like candle-making and painting and, rather like the Selene group, a great deal of their combined energy goes into publishing the radical Christian magazine *Catonsville Roadrunner*. As a strictly 'activist' group, they publicize real and anticipated injustices in the local community, take up actual cases of bureaucratic mishandling, encourage individuals to help themselves in new ways and offer temporary refuge to those who are in particular distress.

The Pilsdon Manor was inspired by the history of Nicholas Ferrar's lay-community at Little Gidding in the seventeenth century. A group of determined friends bought this Dorsetshire manor house in 1958 and set up a man-made family dedicated to the ideals of the gospel and a routine of worship on Anglican lines which offers unconditional friendship to all comers. It has turned into a caring community with a particular ministry to the defeated and broken. A great many find healing through sharing in the whole life of the community for a period of time. The aim of this community is the restoration of particular relationships rather than the reformation of society.

Mention should be made of the cell groups that have sprouted like mushrooms in preparation for the Council of Youth at Taizé in the summer of 1974. These are meant to be provisional, not permanent. For example, six young Christians met weekly at Stuttgart for the study of Ivan Illich's *Celebration of Awareness* and became involved in a fight to save a children's play space among the high-rise apartment blocks. In the Central African Republic a young Frenchman formed a cell group with a number of Africans of his own age. Their regular Christian fellowship gave back the African members their dignity in being black and a sense of direction for their lives.

The charismatic movement in the established denominations is also leading Christians to experiment with the pattern of family. In the parish of the Redeemer in Houston, Texas, almost eighty per cent of the church members have opted to share in communal forms of home life in which several couples with their children occupy one large house and welcome into it as well a number of single people who are disturbed and in need of special care of one kind or another. There is a pooling of resources such as cars, washing machines and prams, and a communal buying of supplies. A new challenge to the strength and integrity of this kind of shared home is now being presented by the arrival of Negro families into the district.

This is only a selection from a great variety of new experiments in corporate obedience to the gospel in the midst of a culture that is essentially alien to it. I am not suggesting that such a pattern is essential for effective defiance of the assumptions of the consumer society, but I certainly believe that these outposts of an alternative life-style are very important to the Christian resistance move- ment. It is easy to deride and dismiss them because so many of the experiments have been shortlived. But at this moment of transition and exploration I cannot believe that this is any ground for disappointment. The remarkable thing is that as soon as one experiment in communal living collapses two or three others spring up. The idea itself is steadily gaining respect. As Theodore Roszak wrote in *Where the Wasteland Ends*,

> Perhaps their experiments do fail, and fail more than once. Surely one has to be American beyond all redemption to think failure is life's worst indignity. After all, the people and their needs live on, and as their experience accumulates, their resourcefulness grows. How can one doubt but that the communities will continue to push their way up like wildflowers through every crack in the suffocating pavements? The tribes and the bands, the clans and the free communes are forming again, even in the belly of the monster.[3]

Many missionary societies have supported their missionaries for a century and more on the basis of a common allowance 'sufficient for life and health but not for luxury or saving', adjustable according to family circumstances but not according to profes- sional skill, status or length of service. The system gives an immensely strong bond of unity and mutual care. When it was being explained to one group of missionary candidates and their families, one parent murmured to his neighbour 'What a pity we can't all be paid on that basis!' Well, why not adopt in at least some close-knit Christian fellowships a voluntary sharing of resources to provide a common basic income and a margin for the work of the Kingdom?

The community in a shared household, the group meeting weekly or monthly, the family working out its own light-hearted defiance, are all small signposts declaring that an alternative way of life is still a possibility. Roszak again puts it most realistically and optimistically:

> Even if one only goes a few steps out of the mainstream to redesign some small piece of one's life . . . it is a sign to one's fellows that something better is possible, something that does not have to await the attention of experts but begins here and now with you and me. In changing one's own life one may not intend to change the world; but there is never any telling how far the power of imaginative example travels.[4]

I believe that the small purposeful commune, dedicated to a particular style of witness, has immense potential today as a new form of missionary presence in many situations that are impervious to more traditional forms of mission. The Spring 1974 number of *Frontier* contained a brief account of one such experiment attempted by three Roman Catholic monks.

> We do not wish to construct a community with a European or American way of life with recruits from there but to integrate ourselves with the local church, thus giving it back its own monasticism . . . We find ourselves related both to Arab-speaking Christians in Israel and to Judaism . . . We try to make the Lavra an oasis of peace. In this 'neutral' territory which gives access to all, Arab and Jew can meet informally. Some of our meetings are impromptu and spontaneous. Others are planned. In both cases they embrace groups from different cultural and religious affiliations . . . For most Jews and Arabs the Churches of the Holy Places and the western religious communities often give the impression of superfluity and impracticability. We must counteract that impression by living a life of simplicity and sincerity. We lived in a tent for four months when we started.

Another experiment which has arisen to meet a particular new need is the string of hippy-style 'families' that have taken the name 'Dilaram' – 'House of the Peaceful Heart'. It would be a good title for any of the Christian communes I have been describing. I visited the one in Katmandu last November. At first sight the gentle, vaguely amiable young men and women who were running the house seemed indistinguishable from the other 'world travellers' in search of drug experience or enlightenment who had found a refuge there. I can best describe their style and purpose by quoting from a recent handout:

In 1968 the first organised efforts were made to minister to the needs of the young people flocking to the East . . . until a permanent centre was established in 1971 in Kabul, Afghanistan. 'Dilaram House', as the the first centre was named by those it helped in the early months of its inception, soon became known for the help it offered to the sick, the stranded, and the searching. To many young people it became what its name means in the Persian language: 'the house of the peaceful heart'. By living together in love as a Christian community, the founders of Dilaram House hoped not only to minister to the physical and emotional needs of the young people, but also to share with them the truth and freedom they had found in Jesus Christ. Since that time other 'Dilaram Houses' have been started in Nepal, Pakistan, India and Holland . . . Besides the normal ministry to non-Christian young people in Holland, a home has also been established there for young people who became Christians in the houses in Asia and Europe. Teaching is given in theology, New Testament introduction, and cults, sects, and philosophical trends. This house is also used as a base to train and orientate new workers who will be assisting the houses that have already been established.

Three years ago Indian Christians were celebrating the fiftieth anniversary of the founding of the first Christian ashram of modern times and trying to assess the value and direction of the ashram movement. Considering the spread of that ideal, it does surprise one to find that it is only half a century since Dr Savariroyan Jesudasan and Dr Ernest Forrester-Paton made that first experiment at Tirupattur in South India. They intended to discover a new style of devotional life and witness, no longer imbued with Western ideals but taking its pattern from indigenous expressions, especially the *Karnatic* style of worship and the meditation disciplines of India. They were greatly influenced by Rabindranath Tagore's Santiniketen ashram in Bengal and Gandhi's Satyagraha ashram in Gujerat. So Christukula ashram came into being in March 1921. Some might express surprise at the magnificence of its main building and central shrine, but this way of life struck a deep chord in India's heart. Some four years later Ernest Forrester-Paton wrote of the purity of their original vision: 'to conceive of a family of the followers of Christ living together and seeking to draw their fellow men into vital touch with Christ first by a life of prayer and dependence upon God; secondly, love one to another; and, thirdly, a life of selfless service.'[5]

A second ashram followed at Poona. Then in 1930 Brother Stanley Jones started a summer ashram in the foothills of the Himalayas. Another on the same lines was set up at Kodaikanal, and a third at Lucknow in 1935. All of them had a strong element of political and social concern besides the inner life of simplicity and devotion.

The hope has often been expressed that the ashram movement might spread from India to other parts of the world. Murray and Mary Rogers and Heather Masterman have moved their own ashram family to Jerusalem to be a tiny centre in which the specially Indian pattern of informal simplicity and inner quietness can be offered to enrich the spiritual forces in that situation of plurality and tension.

This movement is far wider than any one country or culture. As the tides of India's ashram movement and Japan's commune movement meet the new experiments of communal resistance to materialism that are springing up in the West and mingle their particular insights, we may begin to recognize the full extent of what the Holy Spirit is doing for our renewal in these days.

'Behold, I am making all things new' is still the word of the sovereign Christ. But his renewals and revolutions begin quietly, like faith itself. They start growing from one tiny seed, the staggering thought: *Things don't have to be like this*. When that idea begins to trickle down into the structures and into the minds of ordinary people in our affluent society the cry may at last go up: You're nothing but a pack of cards!

# Notes

## Chapter 1

1. Donella H. Meadows, Dennis L. Meadows, Jørgen Randers, William W. Behrens III, *The Limits to Growth*, Earth Island Ltd 1972, pp. 153f.
2. Ibid., pp. 150f.
3. Pyong-Choon Hahm, 'A Korean Comment on the Christian Concern for the Future of the Global Environment', *Anticipation* No. 12, September 1972, WCC.
4. *The Limits to Growth*, pp. 194f.
5. J. F. Rwcyemamu, 'International Trade and the Developing Countries', *World Development: An Introductory Reader* ed. Hélène Castel, Collier-Macmillan 1971, p. 67.
6. *The Environment: A Radical Agenda*, BSSRS Paper No. 1, 1972.
7. Basil Davidson, 'The development of people, not the growth of things', *New Internationalist*, November 1973, pp. 17–18, 20.
8. Roy Billington, *What about the Third World?*, IVP 1972, p. 14.
9. Sir Kingsley Dunham, quoted by Pearce Wright in *The Times*, 21 August 1973.
10. E. F. Schumacher, 'Implications of the Limits to Growth Debate – Small is Beautiful', *Anticipation* No. 13, December 1972, WCC.
11. Loc. cit.
12. John Poulton, *People under Pressure*, Lutterworth Press 1973, p. 56.

## Chapter 2

1. Vance Packard, *The Status Seekers*, Penguin Books 1961, pp. 273f.
2. Jeremy Bugler, *Polluting Britain*, Penguin Books 1972, p. 32.
3. Ibid., p. 165.
4. L. Charles Birch, 'Carrying Capacity of the Global Environment – Biological Limitations', *Anticipation* No. 13, December 1972, WCC.
5. Theodore Roszak, *Where the Wasteland Ends*, Faber & Faber 1973, pp. 441f.
6. Laurence Easterbrook writing in July 1961, quoted by Ruth Harrison in *Animal Machines*, Vincent Stuart Ltd 1964.

7. Patrick Goldring, *The Broiler House Society*, Leslie Frewin 1969.

8. Ruth Harrison, op. cit., p. 153.

9. Bernard Levin, 'Concorde making sense £500m too late', *The Times*, 25 January 1973.

10. Erich Fromm, *The Art of Loving*, Allen & Unwin 1957.


## Chapter 3

1. Paul Johnson, *The Offshore Islanders*, Weidenfeld & Nicolson 1972.

2. G. Ernest Wright, *The Biblical Doctrine of Man in Society*, SCM Press 1954, p. 118.

3. R. H. Tawney, *Religion and the Rise of Capitalism*, Penguin Books 1938, p. 155.


## Chapter 4

1. Jeremy Bugler, op. cit., p. 176.

2. Penguin Books 1963.

3. Samm Sinclair Baker, *The Permissible Lie*, Peter Owen 1969, p. 32.

4. John Poulton, op. cit., p. 103.

5. Theodore Roszak, op. cit., p. 436.

6. Kaneko Mitsuharu, 'Opposition', *The Penguin Book of Japanese Verse* ed. Geoffrey Bownas and Anthony Thwaite, Penguin Books 1964, pp. 199-200. Translation © Geoffrey Bownas and Anthony Thwaite, 1964.

7. Daniel Berrigan, 'Property', *Seeds of Liberation* ed. Alistair Kee, SCM Press 1973, p. 70.

8. See David L. Edwards (ed.), *The British Churches Turn to the Future*, SCM Press 1973, pp. 73ff.

9. J. R. Moorman, *St Francis of Assisi*, SCM Press 1950, pp. 46f.

10. Julius Nyerere, abridged version of an address given to the Maryknoll Missionary Order 1970, *Viewpoint*, Christian Aid, November 1972 (originally published in *The Tablet*).

11. Benjamin R. Barber, *Superman and Common Men*, Penguin Books 1972, pp. 112, 113.


## Chapter 5

1. L. Charles Birch, 'Three Facts, Eight Fallacies and Three Axioms about Population and Environment', *Anticipation* No. 12, September 1972, WCC.

2. G.-C. Mutiso, 'Tools are for people: towards an Africanized technology', *The Ecumenical Review* Vol. XXIV No. 3, July 1972, WCC.

3. 'What is Boiteko?', *Intermediate Technology Bulletin* No. 8, Spring 1973, reprinted from *Botwsana Bulletin* No. 2, War on Want.

4. E. F. Schumacher, ' What is happening to Intermediate Technology?', *Frontier* Vol. 15 No. 2, Summer 1972.

5. Leonard Beaton, *Must the Bomb Spread?*, Penguin Books 1966.

6. E. F. Schumacher, 'Crossing the Boundaries of Poverty', *Frontier* Vol. 9 No. 11, Summer 1966.

7. Richard Exley, 'Otterthotti: one Indian Village', *A Kind of Caring*, Oxfam 1972.

8. Julius Nyerere, *The Arusha Declaration*, Publicity Section, TANU, Dar-es-Salaam 1972.

9. Ivan Illich, *Celebration of Awareness*, Penguin Books 1973, pp. 133f.

10. Ibid., p. 143.

## Chapter 6

1. Andrew Rigby, *Alternative Realities*, Routledge & Kegan Paul 1974, p. 35.

2. The Roadrunners, 'Community Living in Manchester', *Community* No. 5, Spring 1973.

3. Theodore Roszak, op. cit., p. 430.

4. Ibid., p. 436.

5. Ernest Forrester-Paton in an address given at Kotagiri in May 1925, printed in *The Christian Ashram Review* (India), Vol. VI No. 24, June 1970.

# Supplement

Study helps for American readers
by John Schramm and Charles P. Lutz

Bishop Taylor's book includes: (1) analysis, so we can understand our world; (2) theology, so we can see the problem biblically; and (3) life-style response, so our study might result in action.

This supplement offers suggestions for group discussions and a list of U.S. resources for those who want to continue their study.

## Chapter 1

1. Much of Chapter 1 is based on the impact of *The Limits to Growth,* which examines global problems. For a look at regional needs, see a more recent study, *Mankind at the Turning Point,* the second Club of Rome report. It describes the difference between undifferentiated and organic growth.

2. We could all take more seriously the quotation on page 19: "The MIT model which underlies *The Limits to Growth* can be regarded as dead. But the issues it raises are very much alive." Try to make your study of Taylor personal.

3. When the rich define the problem, the *poor* are the problem. But Bishop Taylor quotes E. F. Schumacher: "The problem passengers on space-ship earth are the first-class passengers and no one else" (p. 20). Do you think the problem is our overconsumption?

4. "If all of us decided that our homes were adequate, our cars satisfactory, our clothing sufficient, our present sort of economics would collapse tomorrow. For it is built on the assumption that man's wants are insatiable" (p. 19). Discuss this statement. Is it accurate? How many would have to decide this for collapse to take place?

Does this statement suggest a mode of nonviolent resistance for this decade? The "sit-in" was the form of resistance in the civil rights movement. Is "stepping out" the form for today? But what about victims of the system's collapse? Would it not hurt the working class first? Or, if this system does *not* collapse, might there be even worse results—chaos, suffering, and global catastrophe?

5. Any analysis of this topic can easily produce feelings of guilt. We tend to respond legalistically. But Bishop Taylor provides a healthy and happy dose of gospel and freedom. Look for evidence of it. Example: We have tended to see our abundance and convenience as blessings, but if some things were taken from us, it would not be all bad news. One way of life produces cancer, thrombosis, neurosis, suicide. Living within limits can mean more freedom, not less!

*For further study*

*The End of Affluence,* by Paul R. and Anne H. Ehrlich, Ballantine, 1974, paper, $1.95.

*Mankind at the Turning Point,* by Mihajlo Mesarovic and Eduard Pestel, E. P. Dutton & Co./Reader's Digest Press, 1974, $12.95; New American Library, 1976, paper, $1.95. The *second* Club of Rome report.

## Chapter 2

1. "We need no experts to point out the state of mind, the psychological attitudes, which this behaviour betrays. It is the state of mind of a spoilt child, petulantly greedy and ready to kick to bits anything that frustrates its will" (p. 22). Test this premise against the realities of our lives in the United States.

2. In some monastic traditions, each year a monk brings to the Abbot Father a list of all his possessions. The Abbot Father decides if anything is unnecessary, and it is given to the poor. Try doing that for yourself.

3. Visit a local supermarket, as suggested on page 34. Take a notebook along. Compare amounts of nutritious food and junk food. Observe the packaging used to preserve the unnecessary food. Tell others what you find. List evidences of waste and excess.

*For further study*

*Environmental Quality Index.* Annual assessment by the National Wildlife Federation. Single copy free. Also available in most libraries.

*Small Is Beautiful,* by E. F. Schumacher, Harper & Row, 1975, paper, $2.45. Highly influential statement asking economists—and the rest of us—to adopt new set of values: "the maximum of human well-being with the minimum of consumption."

There are also films available on this subject, many available from your local library. Here are three:

*The End of One,* 7 minutes, color. Seagulls foraging in a dump become parody on U.S. life. Good discussion starter. Available from Learning Corporation of America, 711 Fifth Ave., New York 10022.

*The Gifts,* 30 minutes, color. Shows environmental damage of our way of life. Advocates constraint, harmonious living with environment. From U.S. Dept. of Interior.

*Glass House,* 12 minutes, color. Swedish-made allegory on destructive nature of unrestrained and unshared affluence. Rental $15 from Teleketics, Franciscan Communications, 1229 S. Santee St., Los Angeles 90015.

## Chapter 3

1. This key chapter encourages us to think theologically, to see our economic system biblically. Write a brief "theology of enough" in your own words.

Taylor says *epieikes,* translated most often as "moderation," really means "fitting in." Use this as your starting point. How could we "fit in" more appropriately than we do now?

The manna story in Exodus 16 outlines a theology of enough. You might use it as the framework for your description. After you have written your theology, read 2 Cor. 8:13-15.

2. In group discussion, define the following terms: asceticism, self-denial, poverty, moderation. Which of these does Taylor include as characteristic of a theology of enough?

### For further study

These three books stress a biblical way of seeing:

*The Desert Is Fertile,* by Dom Helder Camara, Pillar, 1976, paper, $1.50. Almost devotional in style.

*Contemplation,* by James Carroll, Paulist-Newman, 1972, paper, $1.95. Four brief essays on "the act of contemplation, which is not seeing some different thing, but which is a different way of seeing."

*Things That Make for Peace,* by John and Mary Schramm, Augsburg, 1976, paper, $3.25. One family's search for a way of living that is nonviolent toward the needs of others and the created order.

## Chapter 4

1. Bishop Taylor's outline of cheerful revolution combines general principles with specific illustrations. Reread the Roszak quote on page 68 and discuss whether the best revolution against this "system of excess" would be a movement of happy disaffiliates. (You might return to question 4 for Chapter 1). Discuss the specific suggestions on pages 78 and 79, and develop your own concrete suggestions.

2. There is considerable debate over whether life-style changes are an adequate, appropriate, or effective response. Discuss the following reasons for life-style changes written by Jørgen Lissner of Lutheran World Federation.

"A simpler lifestyle is not a panacea. It may be embarked upon for the wrong reasons, e.g., out of guilt, as a substitute for political action, or in a quest for moral purity. But it can also be meaningful and significant in some or all of these ways. . . .

"1. As an *act of faith,* done for the sake of personal integrity and as an expression of personal commitment to a more equitable distribution of the world's wealth.

"2. As an *act of self-defense* against the mind- and body-polluting effects of over-consumption.

"3. As an *act of withdrawal* from the achievement-neurosis of our high-pressure materialist societies.

"4. As an *act of solidarity* with the majority of humankind, which has no choice about lifestyle.

"5. As an *act of sharing* with others what has been given to us, or of returning what was usurped by us through unjust social and economic systems.

"6. As an *act of celebration* of the riches found in creativity, spirituality, and community with others, in place of mindless materialism.

"7. As an *act of provocation* (ostentatious *under*-consumption) to arouse curiosity leading to dialogue with others about affluence, alienation, poverty, and social injustice.

"8. As an *act of anticipation* of the era when the underprivileged will force new power relationships and new patterns of resource allocation upon us.

"9. As an *act of advocacy* of legislated changes in present patterns of production and consumption, in the direction of a new international economic order.

"10. As an *exercise of purchasing power* to redirect production away from the satisfaction of artificially created wants toward the supply of goods and services that meet genuine social needs."

## For further study

*Taking Charge: Achieving Personal and Political Change through Simple Living,* American Friends Service Committee, Bantam, 1977, paper, $1.95. Fine collection of helps on the content and process of life-style simplification.

*More-with-Less Cookbook,* by Doris Janzen Longacre, Herald Press, 1976, paper, $4.95. Practical advice and help on simpler diets. The first 41 pages are full of information on foods, proteins, and meal planning. Then follow about 250 pages of recipes for everything from homebaked breads to soybean and lentil dishes.

## Chapter 5

1. Chapter 5 moves from the personal to the corporate response. Use the example of the parish which diverted funds to Bangladesh (p. 85) to prompt discussion of actions your congregation might consider. How does a congregation determine what is enough for itself?

2. Consider your own congregation/denomination in light of the checklist on page 87. In what ways are these characteristics impossible for an institution? In what ways are they necessary?

3. Clarify what is meant by "intermediate technology." Use the examples on pages 91, 92, and 95 to help.

4. Discuss Ivan Illich's criticism of Western aid on page 98. Do further research on aid programs the United States sponsors.

5. The Club of Rome summarized their suggestions under four general guidelines. Use these for general group discussion.

"Regarding individual values and attitudes the following lessons seem to be outstanding for the new global ethic implicit in the preceding requirements.

"1. A *world consciousness* must be developed through which every individual realizes his role as a member of the world community. Famine in Tropical Africa should be considered as relevant and as disturbing to a citizen of Germany as famine in Bavaria. It must become part of the consciousness of every individual that 'the basic unit of human cooperation and hence survival is moving from the national to the global level.'

"2. A *new ethic in the use of material resources* must be developed which will result in a style of life compatible with the oncoming age of scarcity. This will require a new technology of production based on minimal use of resources and longevity of products rather than production processes based on maximal throughput. One should be proud of saving and conserving rather than of spending and discarding.

"3. An *attitude toward nature must be developed based on harmony rather than conquest.* Only in this way can man apply in practice what is already accepted in theory—that is, that man is an integral part of nature.

"4. If the human species is to survive, man must develop a *sense of identification with future generations* and be ready to trade benefits to himself. If each generation aims at maximum good for itself, *Homo Sapiens* is as good as doomed."

*(Mankind at the Turning Point,* p. 147)

### For further study

*The Cruel Choice,* by Denis Goulet, Atheneum, 1973, paper, $3.95.
*Peace on Earth Handbook,* by Loren Halvorson, Augsburg, 1975, paper, $3.50.
*Finite Resources and the Human Future,* by Ian G. Barbour, Augsburg, 1976, paper, $4.75.

### Chapter 6

U.S. readers may wonder if there are "cells of dissent" in this country. There are many. Write these groups for further information:

*Alternatives,* Box 429, Ellenwood, Georgia 30049. One man's dream of a Christmas stripped of commercialism led in 1973 to publication of *The Alternate Christmas Catalog,* a resource book of ideas for Christmas-changers. Since then, two more versions of the catalogue have appeared and Alternatives has branched out to other celebrations: Easter, Thanksgiving, Halloween, Mothers' and Fathers' Days, Independence Day. Their motto: "Working for simpler lifestyles through alternate celebrations."

*Campaign for Global Justice,* 4709 Windsor, Philadelphia, Pa. 19143. Founded in 1976 as companion to Shakertown Pledge Group, to work for institutional/ecclesiastical model of simplicity in which churches themselves begin to renounce their wealth and turn to a simpler, justice-oriented stance. "Pledge of the Church of the Beatitudes" calls on churches to simplify. Biblical in origin and radical in their vision of a new church. Mounting regional direct action campaigns to challenge the churches about institutional affluence.

Center for Science in the Public Interest, 1757 S St. N.W., Washington, D.C. 20009. A citizens' group conducting projects on such issues as energy, nuclear power, food, and multinationals, CSPI has been developing a long-range project on simple living. Publications include *The Simple Lifestyle Calendar, 99 Ways to a Simpler Lifestyle,* and *Lifestyle Index.* Have launched a series of simple living workshops for the East Coast, focusing on practical aspects of simpler living.

Shakertown Pledge Group, W. 44th St. and York Ave. S., Minneapolis, Minn. 55410. Founded in 1973 when a group of religious retreat center directors met in a restored Shaker village to draft a statement of concern about the world poverty gap. The Shakertown Pledge is a nine-point commitment to a simple, just life-style which has since circulated in millions of copies around the world. SPG provides an education/action resource center for the Pledge and simple living issues. Publishes monthly newsletter *(Creative Simplicity* for $5/year), trains "simple living organizers," conducts workshops, and maintains a resource library.

Simple Living Program, 2160 Lake St., San Francisco, Calif. 94121. A resource and organizing center initiated by the American Friends Service Committee. Similar to the Shakertown Pledge Group in projects and purposes, it concentrates on the West Coast. Publishes newsletter *(Simple Living),* and conducts workshops, seminars, and training sessions for churches, community groups, and individuals.

### Additional films

(See also resources for Chapter 2 above)

*How Do We Live in a Hungry World?,* 33 minutes, color, 1977. Balanced treatment of the joys and problems in seeking to live more simply. Presents voluntary restraint in consumption as an option containing its own rewards. Documentary look at several family efforts around the United States. Available at $20 rental from United Methodist Communications, 1525 McGavock St., Nashville, Tenn. 37203.

*World Food: Simplification of Life Style,* 7 minutes, color, 1976. Shows how waste of resources needed to produce food (land, petroleum, etc.) and of food itself, complicates the global hunger problem. Suggests alterations in consumption habits of the comfortable. Written and narrated by Larry Minear, hunger specialist with Church World Service/Lutheran World Relief. Rents for $12.50, Mass Media Ministries, 2116 N. Charles, Baltimore, Md. 21218.

124